BARRON'S

A POCKET  GUIDE TO

Correct
Study Tips

Fourth Edition

P9-DMI-517

William H. Armstrong

Winner of the National School Bell Award for distinguished
interpretation in the field of education and author of the
Newbery Medal award-winning book, *Sounder*.

M. Willard Lampe II

Academic Dean and Chair, Department of General Studies
Master, Greek and Latin, Kent School, Kent, Connecticut

George Ehrenhaft

Former English Chair
Mamaroneck High School, Mamaroneck, New York

Barron's Educational Series, Inc.

BARRON'S

A POCKET  GUIDE TO

Correct
Study Tips

All inquiries should be addressed to:
Barron's Educational Series, Inc.
250 Wireless Blvd.
Hauppauge, New York 11788

International Standard Book No. 0-8120-9812-9

Library of Congess Catalog Card No. 96-19015

Library of Congress Cataloging-in-Publication Data
Armstrong, Willliam Howard, 1914-
    A pocket guide to study tips / William H. Armstrong and M. Willard
Lampe II with George Ehrenhaft.—4th ed.
        p. cm.
    Rev. ed. of: Study tips. 3rd ed. c1990.
    Includes bibliographical references (p.).
    ISBN 0-8120-9812-9
    1. Study skills. I. Lampe, M. Willard. II. Ehrenhaft, George.
III. Armstrong, William Howard, 1914- Study tips. IV. Title.
LB1049.A72   1997
371.3′028′1—dc21   96-19015
                                                    CIP

PRINTED IN THE UNITED STATES OF AMERICA
10 9 8 7 6 5 4

CONTENTS

Preface   xi

1. **Introduction: From These Roots**   **1**
   The Gift of Perception   1
   The Gift of Thought   3
   The Gift of Communication   3

2. **Listening: The Easy Way to Learn**   **6**
   True Confessions   6
   The Most Difficult of All Learning
      Processes   6
   The Problem of Coordination   7
   The Problem of Speaking Rate   8
   The Problem of Working on Your Own   8
   Few Do but Many Can   9
   The Classroom as a Proving Ground   10
   Taking Notes: The Ultimate Key to
      Success   11
   Listening Aids   13
   Listening Errors to Avoid   15
   Daily Exercises in Listening   17
   Looking Back   18

3. **The Classroom: Atmosphere for
   Achievement**   **19**
   True Confessions   19
   Important Elements of Classroom Success   19
   Partnership with the Teacher   20
   The Influence of Your Teachers   21
   Hints on Attitude   23
   What Kind of Student Are You?   26
   Developing Confidence in Your Abilities   27
   Looking Back   30

4. Study Time: Design for Success   **31**
    True Confessions   31
    Your Most Important Tool for
       Learning—Time   31
    Help Yourself. Procrastinate No More   32
    Time is Our Most Precious Resource   34
    Finding Where the Hours Go   36
    Busy, but Well Organized   38
    Making Your Schedule Work   45
    Looking Back   47

**5. Mastering Assignments: Methods of
    Study**   **48**
    True Confessions   48
    Difference Between Reading and Studying   48
    Study Methods   49
    Making Good Study Methods Work   55
    Looking Back   59

**6. Note-Taking: Summaries, Outlines,
    Maps**   **60**
    True Confessions   60
    Kinds of Notes   60
    Format   61
    The Making of a Good Summary   61
    Finding Models of Condensing   64
    The Art of Outlining   66
    Alternative Methods of Note-Taking   72
    Mapping   73
    Suggestions for Writing Better Summaries   81
    Suggestions for Better Outlines   82
    Suggestions for Better Mapping   83
    Looking Back   84

7. Spelling and Punctuation: Hallmarks of Excellence — **86**
True Confessions — 86
Does Spelling Count? You Bet It Does! — 86
General Spelling Problems and How to Overcome Them — 87
Spell Checkers — 91
Spelling Rules and Exceptions — 91
Spelling Demons — 94
Summary of Practices for Spelling Mastery — 99
Why Punctuate? — 100
The Characteristics of the Marks of Punctuation — 101
Summary of Enlightened Punctuation — 102
Looking Back — 103

8. Studying for Subjects: Developing a Feeling for Your Work — **104**
True Confessions — 104
The Beginning of Success Is Interest — 105
Relish Foreign Languages — 106
English Gives Meaning to Feeling — 110
History—Enjoy What You Cannot Avoid — 119
Try Smiles Instead of Frowns for Mathematics — 125
Studying Science — 131
Looking Back — 135

9. Reading: Faster With More Understanding — **136**
True Confessions — 136
The Nature of Reading — 137
Understanding More — 145

Reading Faster   151
Practices for Better Reading   153
Looking Back   154

10. Words: How to Improve Your
    Knowledge of Them   **155**
    True Confessions   155
    Why Study Words?   155
    The Many Qualities of Words   156
    The Origin of Words   157
    The Excitement of Words   159
    Practices for Vocabulary Improvement   167
    Looking Back   170

11. Written Work: The Product and
    Its Package   **172**
    True Confessions   172
    The Nature of the Product   173
    Writing Themes, or Compositions   175
    Five Steps in Theme Writing   176
    The Nature of the Package   182
    Improving Your Writing   184
    How to Judge Quality   187
    Suggestions for Improving Written Work   188
    Looking Back   188

12. Written Work: Style and Usage   **190**
    True Confessions   190
    Models of Good Style   191
    Clarity   195
    Simplicity   199
    Choosing Active Words   201
    Sincerity   203
    Order   204

Selection of Best Words 205
Common Usage Errors 206
Looking Back 216

13. Research Papers: Steps to Success **218**
True Confessions 218
What Is a Research Paper? 218
The Problem of Plagiarism 219
Steps in Writing a Research Paper 220
Proceeding to Do Research 228
Documenting Your Sources 230
The Grade You Earn 235
Practices for Better Research Papers 235
Looking Back 236

14. The Library: How to Use It **237**
True Confessions 237
How to Find a Book 237
Systems of Classification 241
Fiction and Biography 244
Reference Books 246
Tapes, CD's, and Videos 250
Periodicals and Microfilm 251
Computers 252
Practices for Better Library Use 254
Looking Back 255

15. Computers for Learning **256**
What Computers Can Do 256
Writing and Editing 258
Finding Information 259
Communicating 261
Acquiring New Skills and Knowledge 262
Presenting Your Work 265
Suggestions for Getting Started 266

16. Tests and Examinations: The Big Score   **269**
    True Confessions   269
    The Nature of Tests to Come   270
    Attitude: The First Step   272
    Learning from Tests   274
    Reviewing for Tests and Examinations   275
    Suggestions for Successful Review   277
    Taking Tests and Examinations   280
    Summary of Rules for Reviewing for
        and Taking Tests and Examinations   285
    Looking Back   286

**17. Motivation: Each Must Find It for
    Oneself**   **288**
    The Reach and the Grasp   288
    Motivation—Imperishable   292
    Motivation—A Seed Falling Upon
        Good Ground   294

PREFACE

This book is a guide to assist you in developing quality in your work as a student. It explains techniques that will enable you to work effectively and efficiently. There are suggestions to help you use your time properly, improve your listening ability, broaden your knowledge of words, take notes skillfully, master the course content in as little time as possible, study for and take tests, find information swiftly, and submit better written assignments.

In short, this book is designed to help you learn how to learn, to acquire a feeling for learning, and to understand the importance of the things you study.

Chapter 1

Introduction: From These Roots

Learning is not easy. It never has been, and it never will be, despite the fond hopes of every student. Learning involves too much to be easy. It requires *perception, thought,* and *communication*—three natural gifts that determine to a great degree how successful you are as a student and as a learner.

THE GIFT OF PERCEPTION

Perception is the gift that enables you to become acquainted with the world around you. History offers illustrations of men who used their perceptive powers to achieve success. The story of Joseph in the Book of Genesis is one of the world's great success stories. Joseph was a slave and a prisoner in the stone quarries, an alien—completely alone in a strange land and numbered among the dead by his kinsmen. His chance audience with the Pharaoh came because Joseph had a reputation as a dreamer and an interpreter of dreams. But Joseph was more than a dreamer. Had it not been for keen perception, Joseph might have been sent back to the stone quarries after he had interpreted the Pharaoh's dream to mean seven years of plenty followed by seven years of famine. Joseph gave purpose to what he had perceived by suggesting that the Pharaoh prepare for the famine by storing grain during the years of plenty. The Pharaoh made Joseph his second-in-command and put him in charge of the whole program of preparation for the years of famine. Joseph saw with his eyes and his mind, and acted upon the purpose he had visualized. He exercised keen perception—perception that sees through to the end.

There is a wonderful story of a young woman who arrived at a newspaper office in response to a help wanted ad. Much to her dismay there were twenty-two candidates ahead of her in line. A keen sense of perception solved her problem. She wrote on the back of an envelope: "Dear Sir, I am twenty-third in line. Please don't hire anyone until you have talked to me." She then folded the envelope and asked the person in front of her to pass it forward to the person doing the interviewing. The interviewer read the note and continued to speak with each applicant, but the young woman twenty-third in line got the job because of her sharp perceptive sense.

Another story illustrates the power of a strong perception. Five days before an important French exam, the teacher filled the classroom chalkboard with material—verbs, sentences in English, sentences in French, lists of words. She taught a total of sixty students who daily sat in her classroom for nearly an hour. When the examination was passed out, there was a loud chorus of groans. Where had they seen this before? It had been right in front of them for five days. Two students had used their perceptive powers. They earned a perfect score on the exam. The others received grades close to what they had earned during the term.

The conclusion? Perception is the gift that acquaints you with everything in the world around you. It is a precious gift, to be used fully, constantly, and wisely. When you look, make sure you *see.*

THE GIFT OF THOUGHT

Perception without thought brings neither conscious purpose nor action. The gift of thought is the one without which all other gifts would lie dormant. Your whole education is designed to bring growth to your ability to think. That ability will serve you well each year of your life.

The gift of thought provides the human mind with the capacity to deal in abstractions. A sound, for example, is an abstraction that can be converted into deep feeling. It can also be made into a symbol—a spoken word. Man has the further ability to record the spoken word by writing and make it into something visible. The gift of thought makes possible all the valuable things that make our world: material things, ranging from the first flint-hatchet of the cave man to the most advanced rocket; and immaterial things— religion and morals, institutions such as home and community, and qualities and standards.

THE GIFT OF COMMUNICATION

Communication and *community* come from the same root word, and without the ability to communicate, community would be impossible. Through communication you will receive your education, and the extent to which you develop the ability to communicate with others will help to determine the success or failure of your life. The memory of mankind—its total knowledge and beliefs—is communicated to you through the medium of language.

Winston Churchill, Britain's leader during World War II, was one of the 20th century's great masters at the art of communication. His ability to communicate stirred first the British and then the world into action against Hitler. An American war correspondent wrote, "Winston Churchill has mobilized the English language and sent it into battle." Indeed, he had done just that—and he won. When he became prime minister in England's "darkest hour," he communicated to his people what they knew, but feared to utter: "I have nothing to offer but blood and toil, tears and sweat." When Belgium had surrendered, France fallen, and the German army stood on the French coast and stared menacingly across at the white cliffs of Dover, Churchill communicated to his countrymen the defiant and resolute feeling that needed to be given voice:

> We shall defend our island, whatever the cost may be. We shall fight on the beaches. We shall fight on the landing grounds. We shall fight on the fields and in the streets. We shall fight in the hills. We shall never surrender. Let us brace ourselves to our duties, and so bear ourselves that, if the British Empire and Commonwealth last for a thousand years, men will say: This was their finest hour.[1]

It is reasonable to say that this one man did more than any other to win World War II. The world may never require of you such exertion of your gift of communication, but you must never cease working to increase the power of this great gift. In high school and college, the degree of success you attain in communicating what you have learned will constitute your teachers' means of grading your work—both oral and written.

Perception, thought, and communication—these make possible the memory of the past, provide the

---

[1] Winston Churchill, *The Second World War,* 6 vols. (Boston: Houghton Mifflin Co., 1949), 2:25.

vision and dream of the future. And these are the chief ingredients of learning, the basic reasons for education.

The three gifts of perception, thought, and communication, when combined with the willingness to work hard, provide the basic ingredients of your success in learning. By employing these factors you will be able to make studying count for something and be both effective and efficient.

Chapter 2
Listening: The Easy Way to Learn

TRUE CONFESSIONS

"I never remember the names of people introduced to me."

"I didn't get what you said because I was thinking of what I planned to say."

"I forgot the due date for the book report. Did Mrs. Benson tell us when it had to be handed in?"

If these statements sound at all like you, don't despair. You can console yourself that you are one among many. You have forgotten, as have many, that "God gave us two ears and one mouth. So he probably wants us to spend twice as much time listening as we do speaking."[1] You can resolve to change your listening habits, and you can train yourself, successfully, to listen better.

THE MOST DIFFICULT OF ALL LEARNING PROCESSES

It is a paradox that listening is both the easiest path to learning and the hardest study skill to master. Listening must be self-taught, because it is a difficult skill for a teacher to teach. Listening is not susceptible to discipline and is seldom accomplished. The lack of this

[1]*Christopher News Notes.* No. 234, undated.

ability often makes the bore, so well defined by Ambrose Bierce, "A person who talks when you wish him to listen."

Why is listening such a difficult skill to acquire? There are essentially four major reasons: the listener must coordinate his mental processes with another person's, the speaker's; the listener must move through the topic at the same rate as this other person; the listener must follow the speaker's line of argument (even if he disagrees with the speaker's conclusions); and the listener must learn how to listen on his own.

THE PROBLEM OF COORDINATION

Much of what you do in school is entirely within your control. Your reading, your thinking, your seeing—they are all subservient to your will, your abilities, and your desires. Listening is fundamentally different from these three other processes in that it involves another person, the speaker.

If you permit your mind to wander while you read, you are free to do so, knowing that you can always go back and reread what you missed. When listening, however, you can't replay the speaker's words. You must get them the first time. That takes concentration, which means that, regardless of how dull you think the speaker may be, you must keep other thoughts out of your mind and pay attention to what the speaker is saying. Later, you are free to think anything you want, evaluate what you heard, and draw your own conclusions. But if you allow random thoughts to drift into your head while listening, you might as well have been somewhere else.

THE PROBLEM OF SPEAKING RATE

When you learn to read, your eyes control the speed with which you read. When you write, there is actual physical control in your hand. In thinking, the analysis of thought travels at the same speed as your mind. But when you begin to train yourself to be a good listener, you are faced with a difficulty not unlike that of trying to drive a car without brakes. You can think four times as fast as the average person can speak. Only by demanding of yourself the most intense concentration and discipline can you hold your mind on the track of the speaker. This can be accomplished if you use your free time to think around the topic—"listening between the lines," as it is sometimes called. It consists of anticipating the speaker's next point, summarizing what has been said, questioning in silence the accuracy and importance of the words, putting the speaker's thoughts into your own words, and in a classroom situation, trying to discern the test or exam questions that may be formed from this material. If you can train yourself to do this, you will save time by not having to read what you already know. Moreover, you will be able to give more thoughtful responses to the speaker.

THE PROBLEM OF WORKING ON YOUR OWN

Another stumbling block in the way of those who would become good listeners is tradition. Years were spent teaching you to read, and you accepted it as basic to your future learning and success in school. In general, however, you now spend far more time learning by listening than learning by reading. Finding yourself in this situation is probably a bit puzzling. During all your years in school, you were probably told to "pay attention" or "sit up and listen," but it's likely that you were never actually trained to be a good listener.

The distortions that arise from poor listening sometimes cause serious misunderstanding and make effective communication impossible. Sometimes they are amusing, but even these tend to show how little is heard or how easily it becomes something entirely different as it passes from one poor listener to another. One such distortion concerns the words of the Pledge of Allegiance. As the columnist William Safire reports, every day schoolchildren place their hands over their hearts and pledge allegiance to the flag, "and to the republic of Richard Stans," the most saluted man in America. Other kids say "I pledge a legion to the flag" or "I led the pigeons to the flag." Similarly, some children have asked "Who's José?" when they sing the opening line of the national anthem, "José, can you see, by the dawn's early light . . . ?" Another such distortion concerns the words shouted by John Wilkes Booth after he had shot Abraham Lincoln in Ford's Theater on the night of April 14, 1865. History has understood the words to be "Sic semper tyrannis," the state motto of Virginia. But a flagman on the Chicago, Aurora and Elgin Railroad gave Carl Sandburg another version. He had heard it differently: "This man Booth," said the flagman, "he shot the President, jumped down onto the stage and hallooed, 'I'm sick, send fer McGinnis!' "

FEW DO BUT MANY CAN

The late Columbia University Professor Jacques Barzun observed that only the rarest minority ever accomplish the art of listening: "Nothing is more rare:

listening seems to be the hardest thing in the world. . . . In a lifetime one is lucky to meet six or seven people who know how to listen. . . ."[2]

Psychologists and educators agree. Through a series of extensive tests given after lectures, recordings, and discussions, they have compiled statistics that show that only a very small part of the population retain even 50 percent of what they have heard.

Nevertheless, listening well is an invaluable skill. Business people and attorneys, executives and physicians, teachers and politicians, and especially good students realize that a good listener is not only popular everywhere, but after a while gets to know something.

Communications specialists point to a brighter future. Experimental courses taught to both young and adult groups have shown that listening is teachable, and can also be self-taught. Many people have been able to double their listening proficiency in a matter of a few months.

THE CLASSROOM AS A PROVING GROUND

You can teach yourself to become a good listener. On the next several pages you'll find suggestions for listening practice both in the classroom and out. There are also several common practices to avoid. Before going on, however, it would be wise to answer some questions that may be troubling you: *What am I going to get out of this practice? How much will I be able to raise my grades? Is it really possible to save time by listening in class?*

---

[2] Jacques Barzun, *Teacher in America* (Boston: Little, Brown and Co., 1945), 124.

Comparative studies of material given orally in class and material asked for on tests and examinations put the good listener in the driver's seat and ahead of the pack. In one history course, tape recordings revealed that 80 percent of the material asked for at testing time had been presented orally by the teacher. Some of the intelligent questions asked by students in the class were almost identical to the questions they saw later on tests. The percentage for science and mathematics classes was even higher. In several cases, demonstrations and associated material had presented the course so thoroughly that the good listener, capable of taking sufficiently detailed notes, could have achieved a high grade without using either text or source book. Even in English classes, questions dealing with literature interpretation showed that the answers had been discussed in class.

If you still question the chance to improve your grades by improving your ability to listen, try this simple experiment. As the class is being taught, write down what you think will be possible test questions. When testing time comes, see how many of your questions appear. If you give it a fair trial, you will need no further convincing.

TAKING NOTES: THE ULTIMATE KEY TO SUCCESS*

Following naturally from good listening habits is skill in taking notes. Good note-taking requires action on your part: attentive listening, one-track thinking about what you hear, and active writing of key ideas.

---

* Also see Chapter 6 for more on note-taking.

The format and organization of your notes are important. You won't go wrong using the following tried and true method, which applies equally to note-taking on paper or on a laptop computer: Put the date at the top of each page. Write the topic of the day on the top of the first page. Divide the paper into two columns using about one third of the width for the left column. Write your notes only in the right-hand, wider column.

Emphasize important points by indenting, leaving spaces vertically, underlining, or using boldface type or italics on your computer. These are quick and easy methods of indicating importance.

Listen for key ideas, and write them down in your own words. Do not try to write down every word of the speaker; you will become a non-thinking "scribble-maniac" if you try to take such dictation. Notes in your own words will have more meaning when you review them later. Recall of material covered will be much easier, for putting notes in your own words has made them your personal knowledge.

If you are writing by hand, don't erase if you have made an error. Simply draw a single line through the mistaken material. Such a practice is quicker than erasing and has the added benefit of leaving in-formation on the page; you might find that it becomes useful later.

As soon as possible after a class, read your notes. As you read, fill in any gaps you may have left. Use the left-hand column on the page to highlight information, writing there the important names, dates, technical information, or any other significant terms. Such reading is a kind of review that will serve to fix the material firmly in your mind, making study for tests and exams much easier. You should review your notes within twenty-four hours of taking them.

As you read your notes and highlight them, think actively about what you are reading. When you have finished, ask yourself questions about what you have read: what was this lesson about? what are the important points to remember? what might be on the next test? It may help to write these questions at the end of your notes, for they will serve to organize any review you may do before tests and exams.

Note-taking, like learning to listen, requires practice. Even though you think all the material you need is in the textbook or handouts, notes taken in class may make the reading easier by indicating those points the teacher considers important. Note-taking and listening complement each another. To become a good listener there is no better practice than note-taking. To lighten the burden of study outside of class and to improve your grade at the same time, there is little that rewards more than thoughtful, constant, informative note-taking in class.

LISTENING AIDS

➤ Estimate how much of the course material is taught in class, so you may see clearly the value of good listening.

➤ Accept responsibility for gaining as much as you can by listening in class. The poor listener often has the attitude that the teacher has the responsibility somehow "to get the lesson" through to him. It is your responsibility to get through to the speaker and the lesson.

➤ Listen for key words and clue phrases. Key words are those that carry great meaning and so serve as a kind of trigger for your memory. Clue phrases are the words that alert you to important information that follows; e.g., "this is important," "the three principle results are," or "you will be asked this on a test."

➤ Come to class prepared to take notes—with pen or pencil, a notebook or a laptop with a charged battery. If you rush frantically to get the materials ready after the speaker begins, you will miss most of the early parts of the lecture.

➤ Ahead of time, prepare a work sheet to organize your thoughts and your note-taking. Such pre-planning will start you thinking about the topic even before the lesson begins. A work sheet that many have found successful is this:

WORKSHEET FOR NOTE-TAKING FROM LECTURES

I. Ask questions on topics from prior lessons, about which you need more information or explanation. Put your teacher's answers in the appropriate place in your notes.

II. Preview

Write down in the space below what the lesson is going to be about. If you are not sure, ask your teacher.

Take a minute to reflect on the subject and predict what topics will be covered.

III. Notes

Using the $1/3$–$2/3$ format, write your notes. *Write key phrases and ideas only.*

Do not take dictation.

Leave the left-hand $1/3$ of paper blank—to highlight important ideas or to fill in when teacher amplifies an idea.

Take notes in your own words in the right-hand ²/3 of the page.

IV. Question

Review your notes and:

1. Write questions to test your knowledge of what you have heard.

2. Write down questions about things you are not sure you understand, questions you need your teacher to answer at the beginning of the next class.

➤ Make your listening three-dimensional: use your eyes, ears, and mind actively to pursue knowledge. Keep your eyes on the teachers and what they write on the board. Keep your ears critically attuned so you may note what is important in the lecture and what is good or bad in the class discussion. Keep your mind on the topic.

➤ Use what you have learned from listening to prove your interest to the teacher and improve your grade. If the teacher has given more than the book offers, by all means, use it in your test and homework answers. You can be sure that the part of the answer the teacher will value most is the part you got from listening.

LISTENING ERRORS TO AVOID

Almost all the stupid, repetitive, and time wasting activity of the classroom that robs people of the right to learn, arises from actions of people who, as described by Professor Barzun, are "afraid to lend their mind to another's thought, as if it would come back to them bruised and bent."[3] Here are a few listening "don'ts" for the classroom:

1. Don't interrupt in the middle of an explanation to say that you don't understand. If you wait until it's finished, you may have your question answered without having to ask it.

2. Don't be too fast with a related question. Until you have trained yourself to a degree of efficiency in listening, you will often be embarrassed by finding that your question has already been answered.

3. Don't display such impatience to speak, by frantically waving or tilting forward in your desk, as to indicate that the world's future depended upon what you had to say. Before you signal to speak, ask yourself, "Is this worth listening to?"—a far more important question than, "Is this worth saying?"

4. Don't clutter up the thought of those who wish to learn with insignificant and worthless contributions. That you saw *Macbeth* on television does not add to the class's knowledge of *Macbeth.* But if the scenery for Act II, Scene III, was unusual, both teacher and class might enjoy a brief description of it.

5. Don't hurry with that deadly phrase, "But I think" or "But I thought." If you have thought carefully, everyone will know from the quality of what you say.

6. Don't ever believe that speaking is more important than listening. It was Voltaire who said, "Men employ speech only to conceal their thoughts." And Socrates, one of the world's great philosophers, had the reputation of being the most patient and inquisitive listener in all Athens.

---

[3]Barzun, *Teacher in America* (Boston: Little, Brown, & Co., 1945), 232.

DAILY EXERCISES IN LISTENING

All the waking hours of the day provide opportunities for practice to improve one's ability to listen. The requests made by parents that go unheard, the sounds of the world around you—the song of a bird, the interesting conversation of the two people seated next to you, the name of the person to whom you have just been introduced. The last is the one almost universal test of a poor listener. You are introduced to Tom McCabe or Joan Banks—simple sounds—yet five minutes later you say, "I'm sorry, but I missed your name." You heard the name with your ears only—your mind was making a critical assessment, your eyes were busy with the color of a sweater or a hairstyle, perhaps you were trying to place the person geographically. All these things could have followed the initial listening, but they replaced it instead. Here are some practices that will help you develop your ability to listen outside the classroom.

➤ Make a resolution each morning for two weeks that during the day no one will have to repeat a single thing said to you.

➤ Practice selectivity. As you go to and from school, or wherever you go, or whatever you are doing, there are many sounds around you. Practice picking out those you wish to hear. Close your mind to all others. John Kieran, the naturalist, could sit amid cheering thousands at a football game in the heart of New York City and pick out the "honk, honk" of a Canada goose flying south high against the November sky.

➤ Start hearing the things you really enjoy. Do you really have to play the latest Phish CD a dozen times to learn the words? The answer is "No." Test yourself—you can master the whole number with two playings.

➤ Form a team with a friend. Read each other poetry, sports scores, or whatever is of interest, and see what percentage the listener can repeat correctly.

➤ Books on tape are excellent for self-teaching. They are available at many public libraries, or can be bought or rented.

➤ Develop a consciousness of your own speaking so that you will be clearly heard and understood. This will make a profound indirect contribution to your own listening ability.

LOOKING BACK

1. Here are three factors that hinder good listening:

   a. You have to coordinate your mental processes with those of the speaker.
   b. You must follow the speaker's line of argument.
   c. You must teach yourself how to listen.
      What is the fourth factor?

2. One typical listening error we make is interrupting in the middle of an explanation to say we don't understand. Another is believing that speaking is more important than listening.
      What are two other "don'ts" that were listed in this chapter?

3. What are three steps to take after a class to get the most from the notes you took?

Chapter 3

The Classroom: Atmosphere for Achievement

TRUE CONFESSIONS

1. If you were the teacher and had to face a class of students like yourself, would you be pleased? Tell why.

2. If you were asked to contribute to an article entitled, "How to Drive Teachers Crazy," what would you write?

3. If you scrupulously followed all the school's rules and those of your individual teachers, would you be treated scornfully by your friends? If so, how would you handle the situation?

IMPORTANT ELEMENTS OF CLASSROOM SUCCESS

While listening is an important part of classroom success, other elements contribute to creating an atmosphere for achievement in the classroom—or to making class time a wasteland of indifference and futility!

"If a man does only what is required of him he is a slave, the moment he does more he is a free man."[1]

---

[1]Marcus Tullius Cicero, a famous Roman.

Be free—do more than the bare minimum, you will see the results.

Two important elements of classroom success are attitudes—yours toward your teachers and your work, and your teachers' toward you. Another is your style of work—good habits make for good work and for good attitudes, and go a long way toward creating the atmosphere for achievement. The contribution that you make toward maintaining an environment of learning will determine in no small degree what your mark will be. If you are to succeed, there must be an effective partnership between you and your teachers.

PARTNERSHIP WITH THE TEACHER

Two simple tests can give you a sound estimate of how profitable this partnership is in your own case. First, make an estimate of what the class would be like if all the people in it acted and responded in the same way as you do. Would there be a general air of indifference and inattention, or would there prevail a sense of responsibility and willingness to learn? Would the class time be taken up with stupid questions and comments, or would intelligent and well-organized discussion contribute much to all? It is important that this partnership be effective and productive. This partnership may be one of the greatest enterprises of your life because your education is at stake.

Now examine the strength or weakness of this important joint venture by the second test—put yourself in the teacher's place. Is your work the quality that you would like if you were the teacher? Do you respond to correction and help as you yourself would like? If you were the teacher would you pick yourself as one of the most diligent and cooperative members of the class? You may not be the smartest person in the class, but you can be the most responsive and appreciative.

Teachers know that they are not teaching to all the people in any given class. Some are there for the social ride, some because their parents require it, some because it's a state requirement, and some are there because they want to learn. If you were the teacher, in which of the groups would you place yourself? And if you were the teacher, one of the most complimentary things you could ever say about one of your students would be, "That youngster wants to learn." What do your teachers say of you?

THE INFLUENCE OF YOUR TEACHERS

"The teacher's influence," wrote Henry Adams, "reaches eternity, no one knows where it stops."

How you use your teachers is going to influence greatly your success in the classroom. Books of biography and autobiography are saturated with such influence that reached past the classroom into life. Thomas Jefferson wrote: "It was my good fortune, and what probably fixed the destinies of my life, that Dr. Wm. Small—a man profound in most of the branches of science, with a happy talent of communication, and an enlarged liberal mind—was my teacher." And Charles Darwin, writing of his life: "I have not yet mentioned a circumstance which influenced my whole career more than any other. This was my friendship with Professor Henslow—I became known as the boy who walks with Henslow."

Of course it's not necessary to befriend all your teachers in order to benefit from their instruction. Most teachers have earned graduate degrees in their fields, and therefore, have a good deal to teach you. Although having a degree is no guarantee of teaching talent, it is likely that your teachers want to be effective purveyors of knowledge. Although not all teachers are equally skilled, make it your business to learn what they have to offer, regardless of your personal feelings toward them. When students say that they can't learn from teachers they don't like, they are revealing more about their level of maturity than they are about the quality of the instruction they are receiving.

In some courses your teacher will assign you an interim or final grade based solely on your scores on tests and quizzes. Sometimes class participation is also used. In other courses, though, teachers take into account several subjective criteria such as attitude, effort, and even the way you behave in class. Because many intangibles may be factored into your grade, it makes sense to do your best at all times, demonstrate that you care about the course, and—especially in large schools and large classes—show the teacher that you are more than just an occupant of a particular seat. Let the teacher know you as a unique individual. You may well find that your teacher cares more than you think. It's true that for some, teaching is merely a job—to cover one chapter a week from pages 95–130 and give a quiz on Friday. For many others, however, teaching is a calling. They regard teaching as a noble profession, and care greatly not only about their subject matter but about their students. "Show me the person you have made of yourself," wrote one English teacher to his students. "Let me see its full size. For how can I judge what you know, what you say, what you do, what you make, unless in the context of the whole person?"*

Even though you may feel occasionally that the work in a course is beyond you, don't despair. Most teachers respect students who try hard, and they will go out of their way to offer extra help. Sometimes teachers deliberately attempt to push you to your intellectual limits by making their courses extremely rigorous. Ken Macrorie, formerly a professor of English at Western Michigan University, recalls overhearing a conversation between a teacher and a student.

> "This course is killing me," said the hapless student. "I don't understand the assignments. Can't you tell me more about what I should do? I get home, read the book, and start to write my paper, and I don't know what I should say. There's a great high wall in front of me. I start climbing it but then I fall back. I climb again, same thing, I'm never sure what I should be doing, but I want to climb the wall."
>
> "That's the way I want you to feel," said the teacher with his sweet smile. (39)

HINTS ON ATTITUDE

Some of the things that you take for granted and seem insignificant and trivial are actually of greatest importance in making the classroom your arena of achievement. As the following hints imply, the way you behave in the classroom will affect the way you feel and think about your work, and also the way your teacher feels and thinks about you.

---

*Ken Macrorie, *A Vulnerable Teacher* (Rochelle Park, NJ: Hayden, 1974), 38.

➤ Accept that learning is something no one can do for you. Learning is a lonely business, not a social affair. Even in the classroom, in the midst of your classmates, you will be learning on your own. If you expect the class to be a social affair, you are bound to be disappointed.

Learning anything of value is difficult—hard, often tedious work; but remember, it also has moments of joy and exhilaration arising from the feeling of achievement and self-satisfaction.

➤ Expect your teacher to require excellence. The teachers you remember as the ones who taught you the best are the ones who required honest work and never compromised the integrity of the class. They never disguised the true aim of the class behind a front of meaningless give-and-take or the absurdity of useless argument.

➤ Ask questions, but be aware that your questions reveal much about your attitude. By your questions you show that you are sincere in your desire to learn and are not merely "going through the motions" of doing assignments. If you are assigned a composition, don't ask, "How long does it have to be?" Ask instead, "What do you want us to include?" If you are not satisfied with a grade on written work, don't walk up to the teacher and protest, "Why'd you mark me off on this?" Ask instead, "How could I have improved this answer?" In each of these cases the former question carries negative implications, implications of hostility toward the teacher, while the latter question implies a sincere desire to improve.

➤ Behave respectfully in class. Nothing can destroy the rapport of student and teacher so quickly as boorish classroom manners. Arrive in class on time and do not start looking at your watch halfway through the period.

Don't start putting on your jacket and gathering up your books five minutes before the period ends. What would a coach think of a player who slacked off before the game was over? The way you carry your books, your body language, the manner in which you enter and leave the classroom—all these contribute to the way your teachers see you. A little common sense goes a long way: Leave your snacks and drinks at the door unless the teacher permits eating in class. Similarly, don't chew gum, wear your baseball cap, apply make-up, carry a blaring radio, or bring your cellular phone or beeper to class. In short, look and act the part of a student.

Just as you do, teachers like being treated with respect. There's no need for you to fawn and grovel, but to make a good impression, merely be polite and friendly, and most teachers will respond in kind. When you come late to class, be courteous enough at the end of the period to explain why. When you have returned from an absence, show enough concern to ask the teacher what you have missed and to pick up the home-work or other assignments. Like other people, teachers have bad days. Occasionally a class drags, discussion is desultory, students' eyes glaze over with boredom. Most teachers know very well when a lesson seems to be stuck. Make it your challenge to come to the rescue. Ask a thoughtful question or make a provocative, but relevant, comment. If you can be the catalyst that wakes up a slumbering class, everyone will be grateful, including your teacher, who won't forget your effort.

A little observation will reveal that the best students are those who maintain a high standard of classroom manners. They are aware that what is being done in the classroom is to help them learn. They are conscious of the continuing judgment that the interested and devoted teacher makes. Perhaps, save on isolated occasions, the student's only means of expressing gratitude and appreciation is through courtesy—from which all good classroom manners grow.

Accepting classroom instructions and following them puts you in the "atmosphere for achievement." Good habits are as easy to follow as bad ones, a good attitude as easy to develop as a bad one. The bad produce bad marks; the good, good marks. Nothing could be simpler than this. It becomes a matter of choice. Choose wisely.

WHAT KIND OF STUDENT ARE YOU?

How would you classify yourself as a participant in class? In light of the above hints, how would you rate your behavior as a student? Which of the following kinds of students are you?

➤ Would you be an unprepared bluffer? This is the person who attempts to cover up his ignorance by asking unrelated questions or volunteering unreliable information gathered from television and movies.

➤ Would you be the fluttering magpie? If you have visited the birdhouse at a zoo, you may remember the magpie, that one obnoxious bird that could remain neither still nor quiet. A student who is like the magpie interrupts constantly, always before he gives any thought to what he is going to say. More often than not, he repeats something that has been stated clearly and thoroughly already, and he repeats it inadequately.

➤ Would you be the sensitive hopeful? This is the person who has prepared sufficiently to contribute, but is afraid of what the teacher and other students will think of the comment or question.

➤ Would you be the accomplished leader? This is the person who has prepared the assignment, reviewed the essentials, and then established a point of view for possible discussion and a frame upon which to hang the answers to questions asked.

DEVELOPING CONFIDENCE IN YOUR ABILITIES

There are many ways to become an accomplished leader. First try to make your attitude the best possible for the class. Then develop confidence in your abilities as a student. Here are some practical hints that will help you become well prepared and secure in your knowledge.

➤ Go to class with your assignments prepared. While this instruction may appear self-evident, it is all too common for students not to follow it, to prepare little or to prepare sloppily. One way to check up on yourself is to ask yourself questions that will help to reveal the quality of your work.

To judge the quality of your written work, ask yourself these three questions. *First, am I pleased with what I have done?* It is futile to present work that identifies you as sloppy and indifferent. If your paper lacks form, neatness, and completeness, and you are content to turn it in, you are putting yourself on record as a person lacking in self-respect, willing to deal in mediocrity, whose sole aim is to get by. *Second, will my work satisfy the teacher?* Make sure that, even if you cannot complete the assignment, your work reflects sufficient responsibility and effort to portray your desire to do the very best of which you are capable. Follow carefully all the "mechanical" instructions: use appropriate paper, put the heading in the proper place, follow the specific instructions your teacher has given for the assignment. *Third, will my work be judged the best paper in the class?* Others may have more mastery of the subject, but no one can prevent you from making your best effort. Your teacher very quickly learns your capabilities and assesses the kind of effort you put forth. A good effort, even if you miss many answers, is a great booster of marks.

To judge the quality of your preparation for oral recitation, ask yourself these questions. *First, do I know enough to make a positive contribution to class discussion?* Since teachers often follow the textbook, you can sometimes predict what will be discussed in class. If you fear speaking up in class, anticipate one or two topics you think likely for discussion and prepare for those topics. Knowledge will make you secure and help to overcome your fear. You also will learn that sincere and honest comments are not met by critical judgments. You probably will find, with a little inquiry, that you are not the only responsible student who fears speaking up, but that only the bore and the clown operate brazenly.

Second, do I have an intelligent design for answering direct questions? Make the frame for your answer affirmative rather than negative. Do not start your answer by questioning the truth of your own statement. To begin with "Isn't it true?" or "Doesn't the book say?" casts doubt even before you have stated your

point. Other "don'ts" include such introductions as
"I don't know but," "I heard or read somewhere," "It
seems to me," "I'm not sure, but I think." Design your
answer to give your listeners assurance that you know
what you are talking about. Try to make a quick blueprint before you start, particularly as to how you will
end your answer. You will find it a painful experience
if you shred a splendid answer by tacking on insignificant details merely because you have not anticipated a
climax and a quick closing. Imagine your recitation as
a one-minute drama that is to be properly staged; or
imagine that for the period of your individual recitation
you are the director of a meeting, controlling your
audience and speaking so clearly that no one can help
understanding.

*Finally, how will my oral recitation be judged by
the teacher and my fellow students?* If you ask yourself
the first two questions and can answer them honestly
with a resounding YES, you will have answered this
third question. Everyone will judge your answer
favorably, all will judge you to be an accomplished
leader!

➤ Go to class with the proper tools. Take your textbook. If
you do not bring the text, you are revealing your lack of
interest as flagrantly as if you wore a placard enscribed,
"I HAVE NO INTEREST IN THIS CLASS." Take
notebook, pen or pencil (well sharpened), pad for
recording assignments, and special necessary tools
such as compasses, protractors, calculators, and lab
notebooks. If you were playing center field, and inning
after inning went out without your glove, do you think
your coach would keep you on the team for very long?
Imagine going to a music lesson and forgetting to take
your instrument or music. Arriving at a class without

the tools will very quickly put you off the team or out of the lesson.

➤ Follow instructions. Write down, *clearly,* your assignments in a division of your notebook set aside for assignments or in a special assignment pad. Make sure you write down and follow the general instructions your teacher gives about the format for work done in the course. If your teacher asks, for example, for your name to be in the upper right-hand corner of the paper, put it there, every time.

LOOKING BACK

1. You are writing an essay on the topic, "How to Win Friends and Influence Teachers." What are three common sense suggestions you just read about that you might incorporate into your essay?

2. As you examine the many hints for successful classroom behavior in Chapter 3, which one would you single out as being the most important? Explain the reasons for your choice.

3. In judging the quality of your preparation for class participation, you should ask 1) whether you know enough to make a worthwhile contribution to class discussion and 2) whether you know how to phrase direct questions properly.

   What was the third suggestion offered in the chapter?

Chapter 4
Study Time: Design for Success

TRUE CONFESSIONS

1. You have to turn in to your social studies teacher a long research paper on the Vietnam War. Is it likely that you will submit it on time? Why?

2. Have you ever budgeted your time in a written schedule? If not, why not? If so, tell why your plan did or did not work.

3. On December 22 your English teacher distributes a list of American novels, telling you to select one for reading during the upcoming vacation. Will you get the book on December 23, December 29, or January 3? Explain.

   One of your classmates who is certain to start on the book the night before the written report is due explains by saying, "I like to live dangerously." What other possible reasons are there for such bad habits?

YOUR MOST IMPORTANT TOOL FOR LEARNING—TIME

The point of this chapter is that "all genuine learning is self-education." The time you spend in the classroom or lab with teachers and aides is not unimportant, but it can't compare in value to the time you spend alone reading and studying. Group learning can be enjoyable;

you can learn a great deal from your peers, but the learning that lasts and lasts is that which you do on your own. Basically, because studying is a solitary and often difficult business, it's easy to think of things to do instead. To keep mind and body in shape, it's important to hang out with friends, listen to music, cruise the Internet, shoot hoops, take naps. But if you use these activities as a substitute or as an escape from studying, you are squandering the one thing that the great philosopher-emperor of Rome, Marcus Aurelius, called "the only thing of which a man can be deprived"—the present.

The Greek philosopher, Epicurus, pointed out that we ourselves are the deprivers: "But you, who are not master of tomorrow, postpone your happiness: life is wasted in procrastination." Indeed, procrastination is one of the most ruthless destroyers of time and in severe cases can lead someone into a life of missed opportunites and pathetic "might-have-been's."

HELP YOURSELF. PROCRASTINATE NO MORE

Sometimes procrastination is mistaken for laziness. You may even joke about how lazy you are. "I do my best work under pressure," you might say, or "I can't write this paper until I feel inspired." Such excuses may be signs of laziness, but the causes for postponing work may be far more complex and psychologically rooted than that. In a recent book, *It's About Time* (Viking Penguin, 1996), the authors Jack McGuire and Linda Sapadin speculate that the causes of procrasti-nation vary from person to person. Some people are *perfectionists*, so desperately afraid of the slightest failure that they put off starting or finishing a task or project. *Dreamers*, on the other hand, rarely get going because their grandiose ideas are way beyond their grasp. They expect great things of themselves but are often disappointed. *Worriers*, who prefer to do nothing rather than risk running into problems, need reassurance from others before starting projects. *Defiers* feel resentful and manipulated when asked to perform an unpleasant task; they resist authority, carry out their responsibilities grudgingly, work slowly and often do a poor job. *Crisis makers* ignore important work until the last minute, then work like the dickens, apparently getting a kick out of living life on the edge. Finally, *overdoers* are the proverbial decapitated chickens who run around aimlessly. They don't accomplish much although they always seem busy and complain that they have too much to do.

Whether you are a major or a minor procrastinator, there are many techniques available to help you overcome your tendency to put off or totally ignore disagreeable tasks. Above all, you must recognize that you have a problem. Then you can take appropriate steps. For example, pick out a single goal to concentrate on. Choose a small task, one that can be completed in less than half an hour—washing the car or tidying up your desk. If the job you are putting off is a large one—writing a research paper, for instance— think of the job as a series of small steps, each one requiring a limited amount of time. Then, each day for a couple of weeks, devote thirty minutes to getting the paper done. Don't wait until you "feel like doing it." Set aside the same thirty-minute period day after day— possibly a half an hour just before dinner or when you get home from school. After each session you are bound to feel less anxious about the whole job, and when you have the end of the job clearly in view, your relief may be palpable. To keep you going from day to day, reward yourself every step of the way. Treat yourself to some popcorn, listen to some music, take a bike ride—do anything that you consider special.

Another technique that many procrastinators find helpful is to keep a list of things to do. On a small index card write down all the tasks you need to complete during the next few days. Assign each one a priority. As you finish each one, cross it off. Even if you manage to accomplish only a few of the important tasks within the allotted time, you will have come a long way from your previous paralysis. Changing behavior takes time, but if you are determined to alleviate the anxiety and panic that procrastinators often experience, each small step counts as a giant leap for you. To keep up your momentum, never think of the chores you have as burdens. Rather, consider them things that must be done, things you choose to do because of the dire consequences of not doing them.

TIME IS OUR MOST PRECIOUS RESOURCE

There is a traditional way of perceiving time which indicates that it can be controlled, and that way is to look at time as a valuable personal possession. If we were told there was an unbreakable limit to the amount of money we had to spend—that once it was gone, we would never get another penny—it would naturally make us very careful about how we disposed of it. We would do our best to ensure that the finite amount available to us was directed into getting what we really wanted out of life.

Yet faced with the same situation with respect to time, most of us cling to our profligate spending habits. Taking deliberate steps to control our spending of time is somehow seen as unnatural, sapping life of its charming spontaneity. We shrink from becoming creatures of the clock.

Perhaps this is because we associate the organization of time with business. The techniques for conserving time were originally designed to increase productivity, making people into more efficient managers and employees.

So when we think of deliberate measures to put time to more productive use, we also think of being made to work harder. In fact, this is the very reverse of what modern time management techniques are all about.

Far from making work harder, the systematic allocation of time makes work easier. The world of poor time management consists of screaming deadlines, nagging problems, irritating harassments, and unpleasant surprises. Well-organized time managers get their work done with less wear and tear on their emotions and less strain on their health.

The underlying purpose of time management is to spring loose more "disposable" time that may be directed toward meeting one's life objectives. These objectives might include anything from learning to play a musical instrument, to playing Ultimate Frisbee, to seeing the Taj Mahal.

What the workaholic forgets and the would-be manager of time should always keep in mind is what one might be doing outside of work. Possibilities are limited only by our imagination; they might include walking out in the weather of sunlit days and storms, watching the seasons change, seeing children grow and maybe even helping the process along, being there to comfort a troubled friend. If you consistently choose work over these alternatives, then you really do have a problem managing time.

In any case, the principles of time management apply to all of life, not just the relatively small portion of it that is spent in working. Though they are commonly taught to managers and supervisors, the techniques for conserving time work equally well for Olympic athletes, students, self-employed people, retirees, and anyone else who seeks to get the most out of life.[2]

FINDING WHERE THE HOURS GO

Because self-discovery and self-evaluation are the only really effective means of convincing yourself where your time goes, make a time chart of your waking hours for one week, being completely honest with yourself, and record in as much detail as possible what you do. Keep a simple chart that looks like this:

---

[2]Adapted from *The Royal Bank Letter.* Reprinted with permission of the Royal Bank of Canada.

TIME USE CHART

MONDAY, SEPTEMBER 5	

Hours	
A.M.	Arrived at school 8:30
8:00-9:00	Talked with friends 8:30-9:00
9:00-10:00	Chemistry class
10:00-11:00	Study period
	Went to school library—read magazine
11:00-12:00	History class
P.M.	Lunch for half hour
12:00-1:00	Cannot remember what I did until 1:00 P.M.
1:00-2:00	English class
2:00-3:00	Math class
3:00-4:00	3:00–3:30 travel home
	3:30–4:00 snack, telephone, etc.
4:00-5:00	Met friend at Blockbuster
5:00-6:00	Read English assignment 15 min.
	Listened to music
6:00-7:00	Dinner
7:00-8:00	Rode bike
8:00-9:00	
9:00-10:00	

TOTALS-12 hours (excepting 2 for meals)

Time in class   4

Time studying outside of class   _____

Time in social activity and recreation _____
 (talking, video store, telephone, music, etc.)

Time otherwise accounted for   _____

Time not accounted for   _____

Do the same for each day of the week. At the end of the week, make a total for the entire week. Do not be embarrassed by your findings. Be convinced that you can rearrange and re-allot your time to greater advantage. If one week's trial does not convince you, carry the experiment through a second or third week.

Psychologists and efficiency experts have done much research in the advantage of organized time. The results of this research are very convincing. They show the tremendous value in time saving. They show the effectiveness of work approached with a definite job in mind rather than the question "What next?" Research has shown that the energy saved through good organization is directed toward the job at hand. Consequently, one of the significant benefits of organization, system, and a well-worked-out schedule for study, is the power that organization makes available.

BUSY, BUT WELL ORGANIZED

Once you have a fairly precise idea of how you spend your time, you can move on to setting priorities. The purpose of setting priorities is not so much to determine what is important as it is to eliminate what is not. On examination you may find that some of the routines you practice are not worth the time you put into them. Lists of priorities should be checked against a list of long-term objectives. Any task that does not advance toward these goals is of questionable importance.

In the hustle and bustle of everyday life, it is difficult to determine which tasks are more important than others. It is therefore advisable to adopt a system that makes you stop and think about each item. It may sound slightly neurotic, but some busy people use color-coded file folders to sort out their priorities—red for what must be done immediately, green for what must be done within the day, yellow for what must be done within the week.

If we spend too much time on inconsequential matters because we overestimate how important they are, we also do so because of our own psychology. It is human nature to do the quick and easy tasks before the harder ones. We are quite capable of deluding ourselves about what really matters. All of us know how much more important it can seem go shopping or repair a bicycle than to sit down and write an essay on *Macbeth* or study for a chemistry test.

The trouble with doing even legitimate small jobs first is that they tend to multiply, taking time away from work on long-range goals and planning. It is, however, not so simple to stick to the big important things of life because the small ones keep interfering. Crises erupt that distract us from working towards the things that really count.

When faced with an apparently urgent problem, the important questions to ask are: "Is this so urgently important that it supersedes the importance of what I am now doing?" and "Does this require my personal attention, or can it be done just as well by someone else?"

If a problem does prove to be of surpassing urgency, it automatically leap-frogs to the top of your priority list. This means that you should work on it until it is finished. After that, you can turn your attention back to the item that was formerly first on your list.

But here the world intervenes again. It is all very well to say that we must systematically go about disposing of our priorities, but our time is riddled with interruptions. No wonder we can never get the big things done.

The fact is, however, that we need not be interrupted nearly as much as we are. We have a tendency to invite interruptions to avoid having to work on difficult matters. We will even interrupt ourselves by dropping a major piece of work half-way through to do a minor one.[3]

How then shall you design your time in order to avoid all the problems noted above, use your capacities to better advantage with less strain, and at the same time boost your grades? Here are two recommended designs: The first, sold in book stores and stationery stores, is a weekly planner, not unlike a plan book you may have seen your teachers using. The days of the week will be divided into periods sufficient in number to take care of your classes and study periods, with space left over for afternoon and evening planning. In appearance a week's schedule would be approximately as the model that follows, except about six times larger, each space being roomy enough to write in assignments or what to study. Classes and study periods are filled in to indicate how your schedule might look when completed. Along with each class the assignment could be included. That is one reason why a plan book with forty weeks, covering the entire school year, is advantageous.

---

[3]Adapted from *The Royal Bank Letter.* Reprinted with permission of the Royal Bank of Canada.

TIME SCHEDULE

Subject Period Time	Monday	Tuesday	Wednesday	Thursday	Friday	Saturday
Math I 9:00–10:00	*Math* Pages 1–5 Exercise 2 Problems 1–8	*Math*	*Math*	*Math*	*Math*	
English II 10:00–11:00	*English* Julius Caesar Act I Pages 1–34	*English*	*English*	*English*	*English*	*Study* History for Mon.
Study III 11:00–12:00	*Study* Math for Tues	*Study* Math for Wed.	*Study* Math for Thurs.	*Study* Math for Fri.	*Study* Math for Mon.	*Study* English for Mon.
French IV 1:00–2:00	*French* Review Exer. Vocab. p. 10	*French*	*French*	*French*	*French*	
History V 2:00–3:00	*History* Problems in Democracy Pages 5–17	*History*	*History*	*History*	*History*	
End of School 3:00–3:30 / 3:30–4:00	Band Prac. Going Home	Band Prac.	Band Prac.	Band Prac.	Band Prac.	
4:00–5:00	Exercise Recreation	Same	Same	Same	Same	
5:00–6:00	Study French for Tues.	Study French for Wed.	Study French for Thurs.	Study French for Fri.	Study French for Mon.	
7:00–8:00	Study History for Tues.	Study History for Wed.	Study History for Thurs.	Study History for Fri.		
8:00–9:00	Study English for Tues.	Study English for Wed.	Study English for Thurs.	Study English for Fri.		
9:00–10:00	Read, Review, Rest	Same	Same	Same		

TIME SCHEDULE

Twelve Precious Hours	Monday	Tuesday	Wednesday	Thursday	Friday	Saturday	Sunday
8:00–9:00	8:00–8:30 Bus to school Review one subject						
9:00–10:00	Chemistry Class						
10:00–11:00	English Class						
11:00–12:00	Study Chem. for Tues.	Study Chem. for Wed.	Study Chem. for Thurs.	Study for Chem. test on Fri.	Study Chem. for Mon.	Study English for Mon.	
1:00–2:00	Math Class					Good study time	
2:00–3:00	History Class						
3:00 4:00	Home and Exercise						
4:00–5:00	Recreation			Study for Chemistry Test			
5:00–6:00	Study Math for Tues.	Study Math for Wed.	Study Math for Thurs.	Study Math for Fri.	Study Math for Mon.		
7:00–8:00	Study Hist. for Tues.	Study Hist. for Wed.	Study Hist. for Thurs.	Study Hist. for Fri.	Study Hist. for Mon.		
8:00–9:00	Study Eng. for Tues.	Study Eng. for Wed.	Study Eng. for Thurs.	Study Eng. for Fri.	Recreation		
9:00–10:00	Relax and Read	Listen to Music					
	Comments All work finished	Comments	Comments	Comments	Comments A good week Grades up	Comments	Comments

Or you might prefer a more compact model, one that's easier to carry around, and one without space for noting assignments. Of course, one copy of such a schedule in front of your notebook and another copy posted where you study would suffice, perhaps with minor changes, for the entire school year. Such a schedule is usually divided into twelve working hours between 8:00 a.m. and 10:00 p.m., leaving an hour free for lunch and one for dinner. Such a schedule might resemble the model on page 42.

There is much to commend each type of schedule, but many students prefer the latter. Only one day, Monday, is filled in fully. Several things are very important if a schedule is to work effectively. Notice that the period from 11:00–12:00 is used to study the same subject each day. The same is true for 5:00–6:00, 7:00–8:00, and 8:00–9:00. Research has shown that doing the same thing at the same time each day makes the work seem much easier because it does away with the energy-consuming self-conflict and the confusion of deciding "What next?" It becomes a part of you— not a force outside with which you have to contend.

The schedule also shows you there is much time that can be used for the things you want to do—perhaps more, actually, than you have ever thought available. Saturday and Sunday have been left almost blank, but it is very wise to make a sensible apportionment of time for study and reading. If you have a part-time job, you will probably find it easy to allot this time. Two interesting results have been noted from the study of time usage. First, the more one has to do the easier it is to make a workable schedule and follow it. Second, people who plan carefully study fewer hours and get better grades than people who do not restrict themselves to allotted time, but kid themselves into believing that they study all the time. The person who works without a schedule is the one who fails a test and then often complains, "But I studied three-and-a-half hours." What this person admits is that three-and-a-half hours were spent seated with a book, daydreaming, thinking fuzzy thoughts at the edge of the subject but never really getting into it.

A popular alternative to a plan book of any size is an electronic organizer. People in many fields—business, the arts, journalism, law, academia, the sciences—have digitized their schedules. With a handy pocket-size computer, they keep track of their daily appointments, names and addresses, dates to remember, and any other information that will help them keep their lives running smoothly. CEO's, military brass, and high government officials may have human aides and staff members to guide them through the day, but the rest of us need to rely on ourselves to keep our work schedules in order.

If neither a published nor a preprogrammed electronic planner suits your unique schedule, you can always design your own. Computer software, including almost every desktop publishing program, contains grids for making charts for any purpose. Merely choose a grid and begin filling in the boxes. If you run out of space, enlarge the boxes or use a smaller typeface. More boxes can easily be added, using the proper commands. The point is that people who follow a schedule of work train themselves to concentrate. Problems in concentration are, in fact, problems in the effective use of time. The person who sets a limit of time to complete a job makes a choice between getting the job done or dreaming in a half-hearted way for an equally indefinite period of time.

The first of all good study habits is the proper use of time. A well-organized schedule, followed until it becomes a natural part of living, improves your ability to concentrate. From the combined results of these two comes the power of work; and from the power of work, not from wishful thinking, come better grades.

You have the power to bring productive and effective order into your life. The suggestions that follow can make a time schedule work for you; and take half the confusion, worry, indecision, and effort out of your study.

MAKING YOUR SCHEDULE WORK

➤ Give your schedule a fair chance. After you have evaluated your loss of time without a schedule and have prepared a working schedule, do not expect procrastination, resistance, and self-deception to disappear at once. You need at least a month of diligence and discipline to develop the habit of going from one activity to study, or from class to study, or from study of one subject to another, without loss of time or the power of concentration.

➤ Put your schedule to work in a definite place. Place is as important as time in making your schedule work. If you study in a study hall or the library at school, always sit at the same desk or table. Have what you need—pencils, paper, books—when you sit down, and discipline yourself not to move until a certain block of work has been finished. If you study at home, it should be in a quiet place, well-lighted, and facing away from the window. Put all distractions out of reach and sight if possible. Your friend's picture, magazines, unanswered letters, will pull you away and waste your time because you will lose your power of concentration.

If it is noisy at home, study in the public library. The setting, the quiet, the presence of books and other people deep in concentration could help you put your schedule into effect.

Do not kid yourself by thinking that you can study and listen to music, catch snatches of television, or listen to people talk. It cannot be done, and this has been proved by numerous tests and experiments. There is no common ground where study, relaxation, and sociability meet. There is a place for study and a place for relaxation and sociability. If you attempt to make them the same, your study schedule won't work.

➤ Study the same thing at the same time each day. This further strengthens the good habit of action by second nature. It also eliminates the exception—always troublesome and causing some delay. You are prepared mentally for the thing you are used to doing with regularity. Mental preparation is the first step toward concentration.

➤ Fit your schedule to your needs. You know your capacities. One subject will take you longer than another. Learn to measure your concentration span. If you can only work effectively for half an hour, fit your schedule with a five-minute period to take your eyes and mind off the work before you.

➤ Do not be too heroic in making your first schedule. If you make yourself into a relentless "grind" for two weeks, you might find a schedule so thoroughly distasteful as to never endure long enough to appreciate its true purpose—which is to make your work easier and to provide you with freedom, not sentence you to constant drudgery.

➤ Do not be afraid to change your schedule to take care of emergencies and ever-recurring natural variations that arise.

A very important part of your education is to learn to be able to judge between conflicting interests. When changes occur, try to keep the pattern of the day and week as nearly regular as possible. All changes must be followed through to their final conclusions. For example, on the model schedule, if you decide to play basketball Thursday afternoon between four and five, you must decide on time to study for the chemistry test. Not to do so is to find yourself in trouble and also defeat the purpose of the schedule.

These two methods organize your routine tasks so that they take up a minimum of time. These suggestions can help to set you on the right track, but you must work out your own schemes to fit your own personality and circumstances. The exact methods are less important than the recognition that time is your most valuable resource, and that it should be allocated according to a plan that puts first things first. The paradox of time management, as of other facets of life, is that greater control means greater freedom to do things you want to do. By making the most of your time, you can go a long way toward making the most of your life.

LOOKING BACK

1. What are the only really effective means of convincing yourself where your time is spent?

2. It seems a paradox that students who have less time for study often manage to do more studying than the rest of the class. How can you explain it?

3. How would you answer the classmate who said, "I don't make schedules because I know I won't be able to live up to them"?

Chapter 5

Mastering Assignments: Methods of Study

TRUE CONFESSIONS

When asked how they study for a biology test, several sophomores replied:

1. "I flip the book's pages quickly, stopping only on those sections that look unfamiliar, and I reread them carefully. I don't waste time on what I already know."

2. "I look over my answers to the homework questions, review the quizzes we had during the marking period, and spend an hour discussing possible test questions with the brightest kid in the class."

3. "If the test covers two or three units in our biology book, I will read them over, scan the questions at the end of the chapters, and then check over my class and lab notes."

4. "I pray earnestly!"

What do you think of these various answers?

DIFFERENCE BETWEEN READING AND STUDYING

After you have worked to create the climate for study, to allot time and to keep your assignments straight, you must get down to the serious business of studying. Too often people equate serious study with long hours of reading and rereading. Several years ago a psychologist was asked to help Maxwell Air Force Base officers improve their efficiency in studying. As he began his work, he discovered a remarkable thing: "When a number of them [who requested] help were asked if they had forgotten how to study, almost every one replied, 'No—I never learned'."[1] They had found out, the hard way, the difference between reading and study.

STUDY METHODS

There are many study methods, each of varying complexity. They all have the basic aim of enhancing your ability to sort out meaningful information from what you read and to recall it accurately.

➤ A good study method will contain a part devoted to previewing. Previewing is an apt term, for as the student "*pre*-views" his assignment, he is looking ahead, looking for the highlights of the assignment. In so doing, the student begins the process of perceiving the orderliness of the information contained in the assignment. To preview effectively, you should read the introductory paragraph, the bold face type, and the summary paragraph at the end of the assignment. If the assignment contains none of these, you may preview by reading the topic sentences of each paragraph. The topic sentences are usually the first or second sentence of the paragraph and will tell you what the paragraph is about. If the lesson contains review or study questions at the end of the chapter, you should include reading them as part of the preview. By reading quickly in this way, you will be able to gain an overview of the assignment.

---

[1]Thomas F. Staton, *How to Study,* 4th ed. (Nashville: McQuiddy Printing Co., 1954), preface.

Imagine yourself on a journey; first, you consult a map to find the best way to reach your destination. When you have found your map and route you begin to think of preparing for the journey, making sure you have what is necessary to complete the trip. For a journey by car, you will need gas, toll money, and the knowledge of route numbers; on a journey through your assignment, you will need paper and pencil (gas and toll money), the knowledge of the path the line of argument will take, what the information you will be reading is (the route numbers). A good preview, like a good map, will help you to begin to sort out information as you read. It will substantially increase your ability to put the information you read into meaningful groups and will increase your ability to remember what you have read.

➤ The second part of a good study method is reading the assignment. You should read carefully but quickly, reading for ideas. As you read for ideas, you should take notes in your own words or underline the key phrases in your textbook, if you have your own copy. You will find, if you have done the preliminary survey, that reading will go fairly quickly, more quickly than you are accustomed to reading. The reason for your increased speed is that the preview has started you thinking about the topic you are studying and has put the major areas of discussion in your mind, thus enhancing your ability to sort out the information and make sense of it. In order to read the assignment quickly and thoroughly, you must be alert and take an active part in the process. If you remain passive, letting the words wash over you, you will not be able to find the main ideas quickly, and you will have to reread the assignment, losing the time you saved by having done the preview!

➤ The third part of a good study method is review. After you have read the assignment, you should reflect upon what you have read. Reflecting is not rereading; it is, instead, the active use of your mind to recall what you have read, what the major ideas were in the assignment. As part of the review, you should ask yourself questions to test your knowledge of the assignment. You will find if you ask yourself questions, that you will be anticipating the questions your teacher will be using during the following class period or on tests.

Experiments with a group of high school freshmen at Kent School, during which the students kept their questions in writing, showed that after six weeks of practice, they anticipated and prepared for 80 percent of the questions asked by their teacher in class. Experiments with juniors in several schools showed that students trained in a study method that omitted any questioning process averaged nine points lower on identical tests than students who used a study method that incorporated questions.

A good study method, then, employs three major parts: *a preliminary survey, a careful but quick reading for key ideas,* and *a review.* The following are some study methods that others have developed and found useful. Look them over to see whether they appeal to you. Notice that while they all contain more than the three basic parts, each of them has parts that conform to our discussion above.

To make the most of their efforts, generations of the best students in high school, college, graduate schools, and training programs of all kinds have used a study method similar to that originated a half century ago by a renowned educator, Francis P. Robinson. The method contains five steps: Survey, Question, Read, Recite, Review. Hence, its name: SQ3R.

In a nutshell, here is how the method works.

SQ3R

SURVEY: Reading bold face type, topic sentences, summary paragraphs, review questions, will give you an idea of the contents of the assignment.

QUESTION: After you have completed the survey, ask yourself what will be the important information contained in the assignment. Questioning will also help you to link the information in the assignment to what you already know. An easy way to create the questions is to turn the bold face type or the topic sentences into questions.

READ: Read for ideas; especially, to answer the questions you have created. Read one section at a time, and then go to the next step.

RECITE: Answer the questions you have asked, without looking at your notes or at the textbook. After you have finished answering the questions, go on to the next section of the assignment, read it, and answer the questions you have asked. Continue reading and reciting until you have finished the assignment.

REVIEW: After you have finished the assignment, look away from the book, go
over your notes, and get a comprehensive grasp of the complete
assigment.

A variation of Robinson's SQ3R was devised to
help Air Force officers improve their study habits.
Called PQRST, it consists of five parts: Preview,
Question, Read, State, Test.

Here is the gist of it.

PQRST

PREVIEW: Read the topic headings, the summary paragraphs, the review questions, or if these are not present, the
topic sentences of the paragraphs.
Try to associate this assignment to
previous work in class or to previous
assignments.

QUESTION: Ask yourself what is important in the
assignment. Try to turn the topic
headings into questions.

READ: Read the assignment carefully but
quickly, looking for key ideas. Take
notes or highlight key passages in
the textbook. Be judicious both in
notetaking and in highlighting. Non-
specific notetaking is time consuming
and ultimately useless because it
does not organize your notes or your
thinking. Too much highlighting also is

non-specific and does not organize your thinking; you will lose the key ideas in the mass of bright yellow highlighter.

STATE: Answer the questions you created at the beginning. State what was important that you neglected to ask questions about.

TEST: Review your knowledge of the assignment. Ask yourself questions, and answer them. Be as detailed as is necessary, but do not bog yourself down with so much detail that you lose the key ideas.

Still another method is called Four Steps to Mastery. Below is an explanation of its parts.

4S = M
(Four Steps Equal MASTERY)

PRELIMINARY SURVEY: Recall yesterday's assignment, and associate it to the new assignment. Read topic headings, summary paragraphs, study questions, or if the textbook lacks these, the topic sentences of the paragraphs.

READING THE ASSIGNMENT:	Read for ideas, do not read word by word. Turn the units of thought of the chapter into questions.
QUICK REVIEW:	Retrace your steps quickly through the assignment by skimming, looking for the main ideas.
SUMMARIZE THE ASSIGNMENT:	Write, if you can, a summary that contains all the important information found in the assignment. If you lack the time to write the summary, prepare it mentally.

The best study methods will cause you to think carefully about your assignments and put information into new categories. They will enable you to make the relationships among pieces of information stand out and make your own sense of what you read. In making your own sense out of the assignment, you have made the assignment part of you and thus much easier to remember. The study methods also have the benefit of organizing vast quantities of information into manageable groups, so that when you review for tests and exams, you will be studying from well-organized notes and will not be forced to create order out of chaos in the limited amount of time available at exam time.

MAKING GOOD STUDY METHODS WORK

➤ Use your own evaluation to judge which study method works well for you.

➤ Concentrate as you study. Do whatever you need to do to make sure that you understand what you read. Do not allow yourself to go passively over what you do not know; instead, take an active interest in what you are learning.

➤ Study with a definite purpose in mind by setting goals of learning for your study period. If you merely set a limit of time, you will have no way of assessing your knowledge. Set your goals high enough to push yourself a little. If your goals are too low, you will daydream; if they are too high, you will feel frustrated by failure.

➤ Work in a non-distracting environment. If distractions interfere, move if possible. If you cannot move, deal with the situation. Try on succeeding days not to put yourself in a place full of distractions.

➤ Pay attention to all the visual and semantic clues in your textbooks. Textbooks are not written to be read as one reads a novel. They are organized to present a specific amount of material in a definite way. Authors put in illustrations, diagrams, maps, and charts to highlight important information. Authors also use phrases and words such as *generally* and *the two main reasons* . . . and many others to introduce major points. If you pay attention to graphic and semantic clues, you will be better able to identify what is important in what you read.

➤ Arrange for variety in your studying. Try not to study in blocks of time longer than 60 minutes. After an hour switch to a new subject or switch what you are doing, perhaps moving from reading to writing. This variety will help you maintain your concentration and keep a high level of efficiency.

➤ Prepare a worksheet for each assignment. For example, a worksheet for a reading assignment might look this way:

4S = M WORKSHEET

Step 1: *Preliminary Survey*

    a. What do you know already about this assignment from what you have learned in class?

    b. Find out what topics the assignment covers by reading the summary at the end of the chapter and make a list of the topics.

    c. If there is no summary paragraph, but there are study questions, read the study questions to find out what topics the assignment covers. Write a list of the topics.

Step 2: *Reading the Assignment*

    a. Read the assignment *actively,* looking for the topics you have listed in part b or c of step one above. Turn major thought units of the chapter into questions.

    b. Write the page number(s) on which you find the topics you have listed or on which you find the answers to the study questions.

    c. Take notes in outline form, using the $\frac{1}{3}$–$\frac{2}{3}$ format on your page or computer screen.

    d. If you draw a map of the chapter, make sure to allow space for revising and highlighting your map.

Step 3: *Quick Review*

    a. Answer orally the study questions found at the end of the chapter.

b. Orally, recite the topics covered in the
   assignment (it there are no study
   questions).
c. Write down the topics covered in the
   assignment that you were unable to predict
   during your Preliminary Survey.
d. Write down questions you think your
   teacher might ask on a test.

Step 4: *Summarizing the Assignment*
a. Write a summary of all the important
   information found in the assignment.
b. If you lack the time to write the summary,
   prepare it mentally.

Prepare worksheets for your assignments using this
model as your guide. If you leave enough space
between the lines of directions on the worksheet, you
can put both your list of topics covered and your
summary of the assignment right on the worksheet.
After you have taken your notes on the assignment,
place your study sheet in your notebook directly in
front of the pages containing your notes. By doing this
you will give yourself a kind of introduction to your
notes, a covering sheet which is standardized and
which briefly will tell you what is covered in more
detail in your notes. You will find it helpful when you
are studying for major tests or term examinations to
have these worksheets already prepared, for they will
help you study more efficiently and quickly.

If you prefer to take notes on a personal computer
or a laptop, create a template of a study worksheet. As
you read, fill in the answers to the questions. When
you are finished, save your work and print a copy to
insert in your notebook. Then, even when you are far

away from your computer, you will have material to
read and review.

LOOKING BACK

1. The SQ3R method involves <u>S</u>urvey, <u>Q</u>uestion, <u>R</u>ead,
   <u>R</u>ecite, and <u>R</u>eview. The 4S = M system stands for
   Four Steps = Mastery. What does PQRST stand for?
   Tell why you would (would not) use one of these
   techniques in the future.

2. a. The first basic part of a good study method is to
      preview the assignment. What are the two other
      parts?
   b. Assume that you had to explain the preview
      technique to beginners. In fifty words or fewer,
      what are the salient points you would tell them
      about previewing?

3. All schools have many different courses of study,
   and some even have administrators in charge of
   curriculum development. It is rare, however, for a
   school to offer a course in "How to Study." How do
   you explain that oversight?
   Write a letter to your local school's administration to get their opinion on the feasibility of giving
   such instruction.

Chapter 6

Note-Taking: Summaries, Outlines, Maps

TRUE CONFESSIONS

1. If you had to rely solely on the material in your notebook, would it help you to review for your tests? What is the strongest point of your note-taking? The weakest?

2. Sir Francis Bacon wrote, "To spend too much time in studies is sloth." Before you throw your cap up in the air and rejoice about that statement, explain what you think he meant. Can you see a more sophisticated meaning?

3. Samuel Johnson, the great eighteenth-century man of letters, called note-taking a "necessary evil." Tell why you agree or disagree with Johnson.

KINDS OF NOTES

After you have chosen a good method of study, you will need to learn how to take good notes, so that you will have a clear record of what you have learned. You will need these notes to reduce the quantity of words you read while studying and to make important information easy to remember.

There are three basic kinds of note-taking: summaries, outlines, and maps. Each of these fulfills both of the functions of note-taking, but each form is unique. All three assist learners in graphically picturing the basic structure and meaning of what they are studying while aiming at compactness and clarity.

FORMAT

Whatever style of note-taking you use, format is extremely important. Consistency is also important. If you use the same system of indicating importance, such as indenting, spacing, underlining, or highlighting on each page of your notes, your mind will perceive the key information with a minimum of effort.

When writing summaries and outlines, you should always divide your paper or computer screen into two columns, using about one-third of the width of the page for the left-hand column. Write your notes only in the right-hand column. Use the left column to highlight your notes by writing key names, terms, dates, or ideas. Write your highlights when you review your notes.

The left column also gives you space for adding to your notes at a later time. If your teacher gives more information about a topic that you have already put in your notes, you may write the new information in this left-hand column, thus enhancing your notes, while not disorganizing them.

THE MAKING OF A GOOD SUMMARY

A summary gives in condensed form the main points of a body of material. To create a good summary, you must abide by the following rules. (1) Omit no funda-mental idea. (2) Introduce no new ideas. (3) Leave out all editorial or general statements. (4) Maintain the point of view of the text. (5) Write in your own words.

As you are writing your summaries, beware of one common fault in writing condensations. All too often students write down sentences taken from the text, without relating them to one another. Such a grouping of unrelated sentences is not a summary, it is merely a chopped-up version of the original. On the other hand, a condensation—whether it be a summary, précis, or synopsis—is a small composition, beginning with a topic sentence, with major ideas and minor ideas all clearly identified, and with smooth transitions between parts.

If you write a summary, précis, or synopsis, you will gain several advantages: (1) a clear set of notes for review, (2) an improved ability to think and condense, (3) practice in recognizing the main points in what you read (what is important), (4) a good memory aid (your own words are easier to remember than someone else's), and (5) practice in organizing and writing smooth and complete short compositions.

Summary writing starts as a challenge. Reducing sentences to phrases, phrases to meaningful words, will require practice and the study of summaries written by others. Examine the essays in reference books; they really are summaries and are the best examples you can find to emulate. Economy of words can become an important part of your learning, a time saver, and also help improve your marks. The length of a summary will vary according to your purpose and the requirements of your teachers. However, for your own review summaries, try to keep them below one-third of the size of the original text. If after extensive practice you can reduce them to one-fifth, it is all the better. A well-written summary is a test of how completely you have understood a paragraph, a chapter, an assignment, or a book; and of how concisely and clearly you have been able to shorten it without loss of meaning.

Examine the sample summary that follows. It is a summary of Chapter 2, on listening. Note the format, especially the items in the left column.

LISTENING: THE EASY WAY TO LEARN

4 stumbling blocks to good listening	There are four stumbling blocks to good listening. The listener must: (1) coordinate his thoughts with the speaker's, (2) slow down his rate of thinking to match the rate of speaking, (3) follow the line of argument of the speaker (even if he disagrees), and (4) overcome the lack of emphasis on listening as a skill to be learned. Few people truly listen well, many hear only part of what is being said. Those who practice listening in class benefit
up to 80 percent of course material given orally	because much of the material of a course will be given orally, perhaps as much as 80 percent. People who listen well also take good notes: writing in their own words, writing neatly, and writing down only key ideas. Those who practice listening
listening aids	well: listen for key words, have note-paper and pencil ready, prepare a worksheet, listen three dimensionally (ears, eyes, mind). Also, those who practice listening well avoid:
listening errors	interrupting the speaker, asking questions quickly, impatience, making worthless comments, and expressing their opinions.

FINDING MODELS OF CONDENSING

If you have difficulty summarizing, even after honest attempts at practice, you will find it helpful to examine some models of condensing.

Look in a young person's encyclopedia, such as *World Book* or *Encarta.* Read about the history of your state or city. Read several biographies. Note carefully the division of topics, the choice of words, and the use of graphic material in dealing with population, industry, and resources. If you can find a one-volume encyclopedia, such as the *Columbia Encyclopedia,* compare the facts of an article with an article about the same topic found in a ten-volume work.

Equally as valuable as seeing how material is summarized is to learn what summaries exist ready at hand to help you. Are you enjoying your algebra class? Is the study of chemistry proving difficult for you? Are you confused about "Jacksonian Democracy" as it is presented in your textbook? Look up *algebra* in the encyclopedia. Here you will find the course, its principal parts, the methods of solving equations, and illustrations to clarify difficult problems. From a four-page summary your whole conception of the course may be changed. You may really understand for the first time what algebra is all about. Do the same for your chemistry. The enlightenment resulting from such a brief inquiry can change both your attitude, your understanding, and your mark. Check "Jacksonian Democracy" in a young person's encyclopedia, then in a larger one, or in an encyclopedia of history. It is so easy to learn if you bother to give a little thought to finding what you want.

Perhaps you have more than once been in a situation similar to the student who, reading Homer's *Iliad* in poetry translation, could not follow the thread of the story. After much persuasion, he looked up the *Iliad* in the encyclopedia. There he found it summarized by books. Book II, which was causing the reader so much trouble, was summarized in nine lines; and the whole twenty-four books, the thread of the story plainly given, in three and-a-half pages. From this time on, the student did not have to be persuaded to use the summaries available to him. He was able to read the *Iliad* and enjoy it. He discovered that the reference shelf in the library was filled with study aids, waiting to be used to clarify and save time.

Books of facts, general encyclopedias, encyclopedias of specific subjects—history, literature, science— all contain summarized material that can provide quick clarification. Atlases, handbooks, dictionaries of all kinds, beckon from the reference shelf in the library. The use of carbon-14 to explain that Cro-Magnon man's campfire in a cave in France burned 11,000 years ago sounds complicated and difficult. Look it up in a reference book. The whole process is summarized in half a column.

Weekly news magazines and book reviews often provide excellent examples of good summarizing. The table of contents of books, single-page condensations of school subjects, Barron's *Book Notes,* can all be used to help you better understand how you can make your own summary.

THE ART OF OUTLINING

Outlining, like summary writing and mapping, is a learning skill that aids clear thinking, good organization, and the ability to recall more easily what has been learned. The outline is a plan a blueprint of ideas—and not many solid structures have been built satisfactorily without a plan. The outline does two important things with ideas: (1) It shows the order in which they are arranged. (2) It shows the relative importance of the separate ideas.

The standard outline form follows five specific rules: (1) A title is placed at the beginning, but is not numbered or lettered as part of the outline. (2) Roman numerals are used to designate main topics. (3) Subtopics are designated in descending order by capital letters, Arabic numerals, then small letters, then Arabic numerals in parentheses, followed by small letters in parentheses. (4) Subtopics are indented to the right of the main topic, and divisions of the subtopics are indented to the right of the subtopics. All topics of equal rank are in the same column: all main topics on the left, subtopics indented from the main topic, divisions of subtopics indented from the subtopics, and so on. When indented, the letter of the subtopic is placed in the space directly under the first letter of the first word of the main topic, the numerals of the divisions of the subtopic are put in the space under the first letter of the first word of the subtopics and so on. (5) There are always two or more subtopics because subtopics are divisions of the topic above them, and whenever you divide anything, the minimum number of parts is two.

The following examples show correct and incorrect outline form.

CORRECT OUTLINE FORM

Title: The Classical Tradition

I.   Greek Poetry
II. Latin Poetry
III. English Poetry
 A. Epic poetry
 B. Lyric poetry
 C. Dramatic poetry
  1. Marlowe's dramatic poetry
  2. Shakespeare's dramatic poetry
   a. Comedies
   b. Tragedies
    (1) *Richard II*
    (2) *Julius Caesar*

INCORRECT OUTLINE FORM

Title: The Classical Tradition

I.   Greek Poetry
 A. Homer's *Iliad*
II. Latin Poetry
 A. Vergil
  1. *Aeneid*
  2. Bucolics
 B. Horace
  1. Odes
III. English Poetry
 A. Epic poetry
 B. Lyric poetry

IV. Dramatic poetry
    A. Marlowe's dramatic poetry
    B. Shakespeare's dramatic poetry
       a. Comedies
       b. Tragedies
    C. *Julius Caesar*
    D. *Richard II*

Notice that in the incorrect form, no proper division has been made of section I. If it had, there would at least be a section B. The same is true of section II B; had there been proper subdividing, in addition to section 1 ("Odes") there would be a section 2. Notice also that section IV contains an error, not so much of form as of logic. Section IV B b bears the title "Tragedies"; logically, *Julius Caesar* and *Richard II,* because they are tragedies, should be included as subdivisions of that topic. Remember, when dividing a topic, you will have at least two parts.

Outlines usually fall into one of several reasonable orders. Items may be arranged logically in: (1) Time (chronological) order—such as biography or sequence of events. (2) Numerical order—according to size or number. An outline of steel-producing states would probably start with the one producing the most and go to the one producing the least or vice versa. (3) Alphabetical order—a rather arbitrary order used for convenience. For example, steel-producing states could be outlined alphabetically. (4) Place order—according to location. If one wished to emphasize the regional distribution of steel-producing states, place order could be used.

The key word is *logically,* as it pertains to the purpose of the outline. The arrangement of ideas is a personal matter. The important thing is to have a sensible reason for the arrangement.

The practices of outlining for study and review will usually be no more than the condensation of textbook material. This will not be difficult because most textbooks are arranged in logical patterns of sequence and relationship. As in the case of summaries, encyclopedias often provide excellent models of outlining.

Many good encyclopedias conclude articles that cover two or three pages with an outline of the article. These and your social studies textbook should afford sufficient examples to help you become expert. Your greatest problem at first will be reducing your outline to sensible proportions. There is always an inclination to include too much.

Examine the sample outline that follows. It is an outline on Chapter 2, on listening. Note the format, especially the items in the left column.

LISTENING: THE EASY WAY TO LEARN

	I.	Listening is the most difficult of all learning processes.
		A. It must be self-taught.
		B. It is hard to discipline yourself to listen.
Hindrances to listening	II.	There are four stumbling blocks to good listening.
		A. Listener must coordinate his mind with speaker's.
		1. Listeners must not let their minds wander.

2. Listeners must accept speaker's ideas, even if they disagree.

B. Listeners must think at rate speaker speaks.
   1. Listeners can think four times faster than speaker can speak.
   2. Listeners can ponder, briefly, what speaker says, put the ideas into their own words, in order to keep pace.

C. Listeners must follow speaker's line of argument even if they disagree.

D. Listening is not a skill taught in schools.
   1. Most attention is paid to reading.
   2. Listening as a skill is assumed.

Why it pays to listen

III. Much of course material is given orally.

A. In one history course 80% of the material was given orally.

B. In science courses even more is given.

C. In language classes 50% is given.

How to take notes	IV.	Be careful when taking notes.

IV. Be careful when taking notes.

A. Be an attentive and active listener.

B. Use proper format.
   1. Divide paper into 1/3–2/3 columns.
   2. Use indenting, spacing, and underlining to emphasize points.

C. Write key ideas.
   1. Do not try to take dictation.
   2. Write in your own words.

V. Remember those four suggestions for improving your classroom listening.

A. Be ready with paper and pencil, pen, or fully-charged laptop.

B. Make a worksheet.

C. Listen for key words.

D. Write in your own words.

VI. Avoid these common mistakes when listening.

A. Don't interrupt.

B. Don't be too quick to question.

C. Don't be impatient.

D. Don't make worthless comments.

E. Don't begin to talk by saying, "I think . . ."

F. Don't believe speaking is more important than listening.

ALTERNATIVE METHODS OF NOTE-TAKING

Working notes for review and recall may take several forms. Some students use summary texts. A summary text is a one-sentence statement of a section, chapter, or assignment, recorded daily to give a bird's-eye view of the course at test time. Recitation keys are also useful. They are usually words or phrases written in parallel columns. Sometimes they compare and contrast.

Mississippi	*Amazon*
Length:	Length:
Flood season:	Flood season:
Navigation:	Navigation:

Sometimes they merely classify.

Great Historians	*Great Dramatists*
Herodotus	Aeschylus
Thucydides	Sophocles
Polybius	Euripides

One excellent pattern of recitation key is the multiple column:

Who?	*When?*	*What?*
Darwin	1850	*Origin of the Species*

Ingenious and helpful methods of condensing can be worked out by each student to satisfy both need and subject. The function of these, however, will not be to replace effective summary writing and outlining. All have a purpose and are invaluable to the student who wants to remember more, review it in less time, and write it more intelligently on tests.

MAPPING

The third major type of note-taking is mapping. Mapping is drawing a diagram of the information you are condensing.

Many people find it easier to remember pictures than words. These people will find mapping a very good form of note-taking, because it uses their capacity to remember forms and shapes.

You may be someone with a better memory for pictures than for words. Try this simple test. Think of a time in class you had difficulty remembering something you had read. You couldn't remember the information, but you could visualize where it was in your book, perhaps even to the point of identifying what preceded it and what followed it on the page. If you have had such an experience, or numerous such experiences, you will be able to use mapping to good advantage.

To draw a map of a chapter of a text, start with a clean sheet of paper, put the title of your map on the page, and draw a box around it. On our sample of a map, we will put the title in the center of the page. (Our map will be of Chapter 2, on listening.)

```
LISTENING:
the easy way
to learn
```

After putting the title on the page, determine the path your eye will follow when reading the map. For our sample map, we have chosen a clockwise path, starting at twelve o'clock.

The third step is to determine the first topic of major
importance and to put it on the map, connecting it to
the title by a line. On our sample, because the path we
have chosen is clockwise, we will put this first major
topic at twelve o'clock above the title.

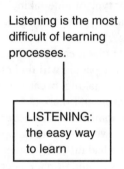

Listening is the most
difficult of learning
processes.

> LISTENING:
> the easy way
> to learn

As this major topic subdivides, draw lines from the
topic and name them.

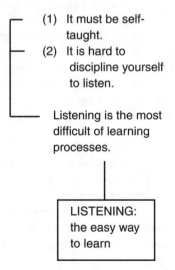

(1) It must be self-
taught.
(2) It is hard to
discipline yourself
to listen.

Listening is the most
difficult of learning
processes.

> LISTENING:
> the easy way
> to learn

After you have finished the first major topic and all
its subdivisions, determine the second major topic and
put it next to the first topic, moving according to your
chosen eye path. Then as that major topic subdivides,
draw lines from the topic and name them.

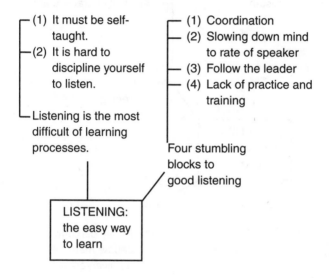

Follow this process for each major topic and its
subdivisions, moving around the page in the direction
you have chosen.

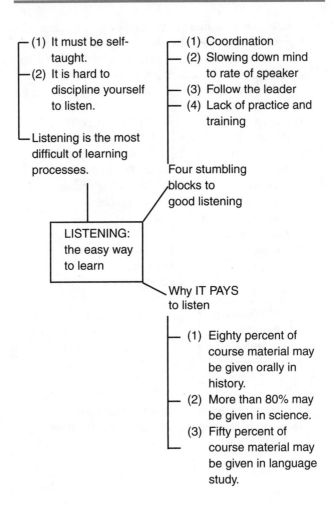

(1) It must be self-taught.
(2) It is hard to discipline yourself to listen.

Listening is the most difficult of learning processes.

(1) Coordination
(2) Slowing down mind to rate of speaker
(3) Follow the leader
(4) Lack of practice and training

Four stumbling blocks to good listening

LISTENING: the easy way to learn

Why IT PAYS to listen

(1) Eighty percent of course material may be given orally in history.
(2) More than 80% may be given in science.
(3) Fifty percent of course material may be given in language study.

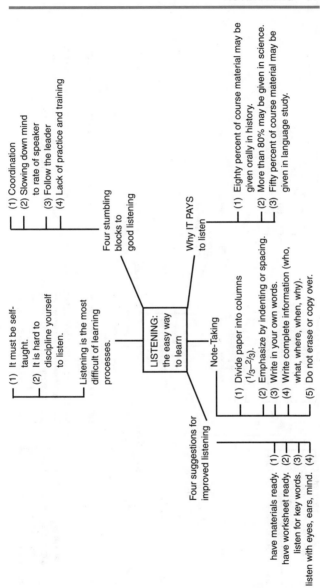

LISTENING: the easy way to learn

Listening is the most difficult of learning processes.
(1) It must be self-taught.
(2) It is hard to discipline yourself to listen.

Four stumbling blocks to good listening
(1) Coordination
(2) Slowing down mind to rate of speaker
(3) Follow the leader
(4) Lack of practice and training

Why IT PAYS to listen
(1) Eighty percent of course material may be given orally in history.
(2) More than 80% may be given in science.
(3) Fifty percent of course material may be given in language study.

Note-Taking
(1) Divide paper into columns (1/3-2/3).
(2) Emphasize by indenting or spacing.
(3) Write in your own words.
(4) Write complete information (who, what, where, when, why).
(5) Do not erase or copy over.

Four suggestions for improved listening
(1) have materials ready.
(2) have worksheet ready.
(3) listen for key words.
(4) listen with eyes, ears, mind.

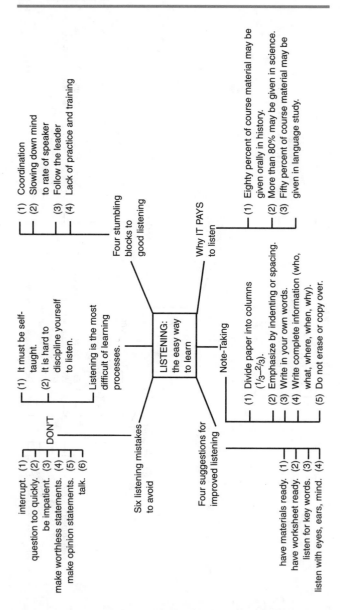

LISTENING: the easy way to learn

Four stumbling blocks to good listening
(1) Coordination
(2) Slowing down mind to rate of speaker
(3) Follow the leader
(4) Lack of practice and training

Why IT PAYS to listen
(1) Eighty percent of course material may be given orally in history.
(2) More than 80% may be given in science.
(3) Fifty percent of course material may be given in language study.

Note-Taking
(1) Divide paper into columns (1/3–2/3).
(2) Emphasize by indenting or spacing.
(3) Write in your own words.
(4) Write complete information (who, what, where, when, why).
(5) Do not erase or copy over.

Four suggestions for improved listening
(1) have materials ready.
(2) have worksheet ready.
(3) listen for key words.
(4) listen with eyes, ears, mind.

Six listening mistakes to avoid
DON'T
(1) interrupt.
(2) question too quickly.
(3) be impatient.
(4) make worthless statements.
(5) make opinion statements.
(6) talk.

Listening is the most difficult of learning processes.
(1) It must be self-taught.
(2) It is hard to discipline yourself to listen.

Our map of Chapter 2 reaches its final form with the addition of the sixth major topic and its subdivisions (see page 78).

Mapping may take any form you wish—feel free to use whatever shapes you find make sense to you. You may use colors to code the areas, or you may use any eye path that is comfortable for you. On page 80 is another map of Chapter 2, using a different eye path. Read this one from left to right. Which of the maps is easier for you to use?

You need not make such spidery things as our sample maps. Many people have great success using overlapping circles or geometric shapes—triangles for three part ideas, squares for four, and so on. The only object of a map is to present information clearly to you, so that you can understand and remember easily what you have read.

Mapping may be used for notes from lectures as well as for notes from reading. Try this type of note-taking, particularly if you have a good visual memory. With a little practice, you will find that it can be very helpful.

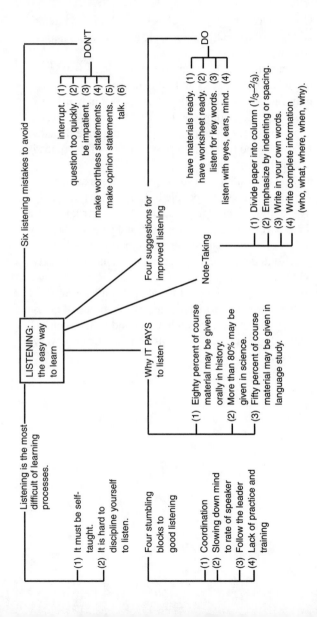

Listening is the most difficult of learning processes.

(1) It must be self-taught.
(2) It is hard to discipline yourself to listen.

Four stumbling blocks to good listening

(1) Coordination
(2) Slowing down mind to rate of speaker
(3) Follow the leader
(4) Lack of practice and training

LISTENING: the easy way to learn

Six listening mistakes to avoid

DON'T
(1) interrupt.
(2) question too quickly.
(3) be impatient.
(4) make worthless statements.
(5) make opinion statements.
(6) talk.

Four suggestions for improved listening

DO
(1) have materials ready.
(2) have worksheet ready.
(3) listen for key words.
(4) listen with eyes, ears, mind.

Note-Taking

(1) Divide paper into column ($1/3$–$2/3$).
(2) Emphasize by indenting or spacing.
(3) Write in your own words.
(4) Write complete information (who, what, where, when, why).

Why IT PAYS to listen

(1) Eighty percent of course material may be given orally in history.
(2) More than 80% may be given in science.
(3) Fifty percent of course material may be given in language study.

SUGGESTIONS FOR WRITING BETTER SUMMARIES

➤ Get into the habit of summarizing what you read and study. Use pleasurable reading—newspapers, magazines, stories—as your training ground for studying and reading for school. Whatever you read, try visualizing how you might summarize it. The more you practice, the easier summary writing gets. When you can quickly summarize what other hardly grasp, think how you can impress your teachers and friends.

➤ Train yourself to replace the author's words with your own, but not just an equivalent word. Try to select an equally impressive synonym or a better one. This makes your summary so personal that recall is almost automatic.

➤ Practice economy of words. Link parallel details together. Use the semicolon to emphasize in one sentence what is expressed in the original text in three. Learn to link ideas in series for easy recall. Practicing economy of words is an aid to separating main points from nonessential introductory and illustrative material.

➤ Avoid generalizing in your summaries. Avoid unnecessary lead-ins and repetitive conclusions. Differentiate between fact and opinion. If you happen to be writing about the end of the Cold War, there's no need to remind yourself (or your teacher) that Russia was an adversary of the United States and its allies. That fact is too well-known and obvious to state in a concise summary. Nor do you need to say that the Soviet Union was the evil empire and deserved to be defeated. That may be your opinion, but if the idea does not appear in the material you're summarizing, leave it out.

➤ Learn to distinguish between fragmentation and summarization. Fragmentation is bringing together ideas from an assignment and recording them in a haphazard manner. A good summary is a miniature theme containing all the elements—unity, coherence, and emphasis.

➤ Do not content yourself with reading one or two summaries and accepting them as models. Compare the summaries you write with ones on similar topics in encyclopedias. The reference shelf in a library is a good storehouse of models.

➤ When you write your summaries, make sure that you follow the $\frac{1}{3} - \frac{2}{3}$ format on the page, saving the left-hand column for highlighting when you review your notes.

SUGGESTIONS FOR BETTER OUTLINES

➤ Observe carefully the standard outline form. Any changes, transpositions, or incorrect indentations may show evidence of sloppy thinking and a weak grasp of the subject.

➤ Avoid the most common error in outlining—leaving off the title or designating it as a main topic.

➤ Be sure your outline clearly shows: (1) the arrangement of ideas; and (2) the relative importance of the ideas.

➤ Remember that a subtopic results from division of a topic. Therefore, there will always be at least two subtopics—*A* and *B, 1* and *2, a* and *b*. Nothing that is divided can remain whole (one); it will become two, three, etc., depending upon its separate parts.

➤ Know the orders of outlines: (1) time, (2) numerical, (3) alphabetical, and (4) place. Use common sense to give ideas the most sensible arrangement. If you can reasonably explain the order you have used, your outline is probably in good order.

➤ Use the outline as an aid to memory, a blueprint for easy recall, an organizational frame for written tests and themes, and a time-saver at exam time.

➤ Make sure to use the $\frac{1}{3} - \frac{2}{3}$ format for your outline, leaving the left-hand column for highlighting when you review.

SUGGESTIONS FOR BETTER MAPPING

➤ Plan your map ahead of time. For example, will it contain radiating lines, or will it look like a wall of building blocks?

➤ Use shapes that are meaningful—triangles are good for three-part ideas, concentric circles for sets and subsets, octagons for things not to do, since we associate that shape with stop signs.

➤ Use color coding if you can—one topic completely in blue, another in red, another in black, and so forth.

➤ Make sure the units of the map are distinct and clearly separated from one another.

➤ Write the words so that you need not rotate the paper to read them.

LOOKING BACK

1. These notes from World History 104 were found in a student's notebook. They deal with a lesson on Mao Zedong, the powerful Chinese leader of post-World War II. As you examine them, point out (a) their strengths, (b) their weaknesses; then suggest ways in which the notes could be improved.

World History 104   _February 9_

Mao Zedong

- ambitious for country's growth
- looked in four different directions: Korea, Vietnam, Tibet, Nationalist China
- North Korea / U.S.
- Foothold after Armistice
- Mao was a veritable thorn in the side of the United States when it came to Vietnam. He sent arms, soldiers, and officers to help the Communist Vietnamese combat the French and then the United States.
- Tibet conquest - gateway India
- First "protest"
- Attack religion
- Takeover followed
- Taiwan ever since 1949
- American fleet a headache

---

2. According to a friend of yours, "Mr. Reardon always asks for an outline along with our English compositions. I write the composition first, then make up the outline for old Reardon. He never gets wise to my short cut!"

   How good is that technique? Before you answer, try it out both ways—writing the outline before and after you do your next writing assignment.

Chapter 7

Spelling and Punctuation: Hallmarks of Excellence

TRUE CONFESSIONS

1. "When I was in elementary school," a famous novelist said, "I used to throw up out of fear every Friday morning because that was the day for the weekly spelling test."

   Why might a spelling test hold such terrors for a student? Are you confident about your spelling ability? Are you embarrassed by spelling errors you make?

2. "I think it's foolish to waste so much time on spelling. Today we have spell checkers and electronic gadgets of all kinds that can correct our mistakes for us."

   What is your opinion of this student's statement?

3. "Marge," said Joan, "is a meathead."
   "Marge said Joan is a meathead."

   Who is the meathead? What important observation regarding punctuation can we make from examining these two short sentences?

DOES SPELLING COUNT? YOU BET IT DOES!

Face it, spelling counts. Whether it's fair or not, the quality of your writing will be judged by how accurately you can spell. In class as well as on standardized essay tests like the SAT II: Writing, poor spelling will adversely affect your grade. Good spellers don't earn extra credit for avoiding errors but poor spellers lose credit for making them.

Similarly, poor punctuation leaves a negative impression on readers, particularly when erratic punctuation interferes with the clarity of the writing. A mere comma can make the difference. Notice what the absence of commas does to the clarity of these two sentences.

> While Karen was riding her bike got a flat tire.

> Jeff left alone for the weekend invited his friends to a party.

A great deal of hard work and effort may fall to pieces if you fail to spell and punctuate properly.

GENERAL SPELLING PROBLEMS AND HOW TO OVERCOME THEM

Many people make most of their mistakes by misspelling the same few words over and over. If this describes you, a remedy is at hand if you are willing to work at it.

First, keep a list of words you misspell most frequently. When you add a word to the list, illuminate the part of the word you misspell by capitalizing the letters you miss most often.

apitude	apTitude
seperate	sepArate
privelege	privIlege
litrature	litErature
Febuary	FebRuary
boundry	boundAry
ocassionaly	oCCaSionaLLy

Second, go over this list orally from time to time. Then close your eyes, and visualize the trouble spots in capital letters. Open your eyes, and repeat the list; then close them, and visualize the word in small letters, as they would appear on the printed page. Then write the list correctly several times.

One of the most common spelling problems is transposing letters, as in *villian* (villain) and *pyschology* (psychology). If you can recognize errors such as these when you reread what you have written, you will improve your spelling by merely paying closer attention to each word. When you have completed a paper or essay, proofread slowly and carefully. But read it backwards. By reading right to left, your eye will pause on each word, enabling you to catch errors that you might miss reading the words in normal order. You might also correct this kind of error by keeping a list of words you commonly misspell. Head the list *Personal Spelling Demons* and review it frequently. After a while, the demons may vanish from your writing.

Some spelling errors spring from mispronouncing words. Many educated people, for example, say *jewl-er-y* instead of *jew-el-ry* and *real-a-tor* instead of *re-al-tor*. Even former President Jimmy Carter, at one time the skipper of an atomic submarine, has been heard to say *nuc-u-lar* instead of *nuc-le-ar*. Dropping and adding syllables to the spoken word may also lead to spelling mistakes.

You will find that pronouncing words carefully and correctly will help your spelling, even though many English words are not spelled phonetically (according to sound). You may find it helpful to underline the syllables you add or omit.

labratory	lab*o*ratory
practicly	practic*all*y

disasterous	disastrous
rememberance	remembrance
hinderance	hindrance
enterance	entrance
intrest	interest

Other poor spellers have difficulty with homonyms. "Homonym" comes from the Greek words *homos*, meaning same, and *onoma,* meaning name—thus, "homonym" means same name. Homonyms are words that have the same name (sound) but different meaning and spelling, such as *to, too, two—right, write, rite, wright—you, yew, ewe*—and *pair, pare, pear.*

You can correct this all too common spelling fault by learning homonyms and their meanings. Some of the ones most often misused follow:

aloud	born	compliment
allowed	borne	complement
altogether	bough	council
all together	bow	counsel
all ready	brake	decent
already	break	descent
alter	by	dual
altar	buy	duel
assent	canon	desert
ascent	cannon	dessert
advice	capitol	dear
advise	capital	deer
bare	coarse	fair
bear	course	fare
berth	corps	forth
birth	corpse	fourth

goal	meat	shown
gold	meet	shone
grown	made	steal
groan	maid	steel
hear	mist	steak
here	missed	stake
heir	pail	stationary
air	pale	stationery
heal	peace	son
heel	piece	sun
him	peal	tale
hymn	peel	tail
hole	plain	there
whole	plane	their
		they're
herd	pour	
heard	pore	to
		too
knew	principal	two
new	principle	
		threw
lesson	profit	through
lessen	prophet	
		write
led	seam	right
lead (metal)	seem	rite
		weather
		whether

SPELL CHECKERS

Because of the advent of spell checkers in most word processing programs, some people claim that accurate spelling has become an obsolete art. Don't believe it. Computer spell checkers do a wonderful job, but they have severe limitations. For one, they don't contain every word you are likely to use in your writing. A built-in dictionary of, say, 50,000 words may sound like an ample selection, but your mind is capable of devising perfectly acceptable variations of words that dictionary writers never thought to include in spelling programs. A more serious limitation, however, is the inability of spell checkers to single out misused words. For example, in this sentence—*The angel is ninety degrees*—every word is correctly spelled, but still the sentence contains a spelling error: *angel* should be *angle*. In other words, you can't depend on spell checkers to identify properly spelled words that are incorrect in a particular context. You, as the writer, still have to know when to use *there, they're* and *their*, as well as *through* and *threw,* and scores of other homonyms. In short, when it comes to spelling, you are smarter than your computer.

SPELLING RULES AND EXCEPTIONS

At some time in your schooling you may have been taught the basic spelling rules of English. If you haven't used them regularly, you may have forgotten them, or perhaps you were absent on the day they were taught. Here, to refresh your memory, are several helpful rules that, when followed, are very likely to improve your spelling:

➤ Words that contain *ei* and *ie* follow a two-part rule.

  (a) Write *i* before *e* except after *c*.

ie	*ei*
bel*ie*ve	rece*i*ve
rel*ie*f	rece*i*pt
ach*ie*ve	c*ei*ling

(b) Write *ei* when the sound is *a*

    weigh (way), neighbor (nāber), freight (frāt).

Some exceptions are:

    either, weird, leisure, seize, protein.

➤ When a suffix beginning with a vowel (able, ance, ed, ing, ist) is added, double the final consonant if the consonant is preceded by a single vowel that is accented.

begi*nn*ing	acqui*tt*ed
refe*rr*ing	occu*rr*ed
commi*tt*ed	occu*rr*ence
expe*ll*ed	allo*tt*ed
dru*gg*ist	swi*mm*ing

Exceptions occur when the suffix changes the accent.

    transfe*rr*ed (transfe*r*able)
    prefe*rr*ing (prefe*r*ence)
    refe*rr*ed (refe*r*ence)

Exceptions also result from alternate accepted spellings.

    trave*l*ing (trave*ll*ing)
    worshi*p*ing (worshi*pp*ing)
    paralle*l*ed (paralle*ll*ed)

➤ Words that end in a silent *e* drop the *e* if a suffix beginning with a vowel is added.

come—coming	dine—dining
desire—desirable	force—forcing
believe—believable	debate—debating

Exceptions occur in words ending in *ce* and *ge* when the suffix begins with *a* or *o*.

peaceable, noticeable, courageous, serviceable.

Exceptions also occur with some words ending in *e* when the suffix begins with a consonant.

whole (wholly)
true (truly)
awe (awful)
judge (judgment)

➤ Words that end in *y* after a consonant change the *y* to *i* when suffixes are added, except when those suffixes begin with *i*.

try—tries	carry—carries
dry—dries	apply—applies
vary—varied	notify—notified

Examples of suffix beginning with *i*:

try—trying	rely—relying
worry—worrying	dry—drying
pity—pitying	

➤ Words ending in *y* change the *y* to *i* for the *ly* suffix; those ending in *e,* except *le*, also add *ly*.

Examples of **y** to **i**:

lazy—lazily	merry—merrily
temporary—temporarily	steady—steadily
satisfactory—satisfactorily	ordinary—ordinarily
late—lately	extreme—extremely
sincere—sincerely	definite—definitely

Exceptions occur when words end in *le*. The *e* is dropped and *y* added:

able—ably	gentle—gently
audible—audibly	subtle—subtly
reliable—reliably	double—doubly

➤ Words ending in *l* add *ly*.

personal—personally	hopeful—hopefully
usual—usually	cruel—cruelly
awful—awfully	oral—orally

There are other rules and other exceptions, but this half dozen will help you form better habits of spelling.

SPELLING DEMONS

What follows is a list of words most often misspelled by high school students. As you study them, visualize how they are most frequently misspelled.

SIMPLE WORDS OFTEN MISSPELLED

ache	can't	easy
again	choose (present	enough
always	tense; *chose*	every
among	is past tense)	February
answer	color	forty
any	coming	friend
been	cough	grammar
beginning	could	guess
believe	country	half
blue	dear	having
break (to shatter)	doctor	hear (ear)
built	does	heard
business	done	here (*there*—a
busy	don't	place)
buy	early	

hoarse (frog in your throat)
hour
instead
just
knew
know
laid
loose (adjective and verb)
lose (verb—to *lose* money)

making
many
meant
minute
much
none
often
once
piece (a part of something)
raise

read (spelling is same for all tenses)
ready
said
says
seems
separate
shepherd
shoes
since
some

Make a list of your own, starting with spelling demons from the preceding selection. Add words you commonly misspell until you have reached three hundred. If you master your troublesome list of three hundred, you will probably be a better than average speller for the rest of your life. You will have evaluated your faults and developed habits to correct them.

When you have compiled your own list of three hundred, compare it with the following. The spelling demons that follow were misspelled most often on papers in a five-year test conducted at Kent School, Kent, Connecticut.

A
absence
accidentally
accommodate
accumulate
achievement
acknowledge
acquaintance
across

advice (noun)
advise (verb)
aggravate
all right
altogether
always
among
analysis
apparent

appearance
appropriate
arctic
argument
arrangement
ascend
assistant
association
athletics

audience
auxiliary
awful
awkward

B
beautiful
beginning
believe
benefit
boundary
breathe
bureau
business

C
calendar
campaign
candidate
captain
cemetery
certain
changeable
college
coming
committee
comparatively
completely
conceive
conquer
conscience
conscious
convenience
convenient

copies
courageous
courteous
criticism
criticize
crowd
curiosity

D
defense
definite
describe
description
desirable
despair
desperate
develop
dining
disappear
disappoint
disastrous
discipline
disease
dissatisfied
divide
doctor
doesn't

E
ectasy
efficient
eighth
embarrass
equipped

especially
exaggerate
excellent
exercise
exhaust
existence
explanation
extraordinary

F
familiar
fascinate
fatigue
February
finally
foreign
forty
fourth
friend
fulfill

G
generally
genius
government
governor
grammar
grateful
grievous
guarantee
guard
guardian
gymnasium

H

handkerchief
harass
height
heroes
hindrance
hoping
horizon
hospital
hurriedly
hypocrisy

I

imagination
immediately
incidentally
independent
indispensable
infinite
initial
instance
intelligence
interest
interpret
irresistible
its

J

judgment

K

knowledge

L

laboratory
leisure
liable
license
lightning
likely
literature
loneliness
lonely
lose
lying

M

maintain
maintenance
maneuver
manual
marriage
mathematics
meant
medicine
medieval
merely
miniature
minimum
minute
mischievous
misspelled
movable
muscle
mysterious

N

necessary
necessity
neither
nickel
niece
nineteen
ninety
ninth
noticeable
nuisance

O

obedience
occasion
occasionally
occurred
occurrence
omission
omitted
opinion
opportunity
optimism
optimistic
orchestra
original
outrageous

P

pamphlet
parallel
parliament
particularly

pastime
peaceable
perceive
perform
perhaps
permanent
permissible
personally
personnel
perspiration
persuade
physician
picnic
planning
portrait
portray
possess
possibility
practically
preceding
preferred
prejudice
privilege
probably
procedure
proceed
professor
pronunciation
purpose
pursue

Q
quantity
quiet

quite

R
realize
really
receive
recognize
recommend
referred
reign
relief
religious
repetition
representative
restaurant
rhythm
ridiculous
roommate

S
safety
satisfactorily
schedule
secretary
seize
sentence
separate
shining
siege
similar
sincerely
sophomore
specimen
speech

strength
strenuous
stretch
studying
subtle
succeed
success
successful
sufficient
supersede
superior
surely
surprise
syllable

T
tariff
temperament
thorough
thoroughly
tragedy
tremendous
truly
tyranny
Tuesday
twelfth

U
unanimous
undoubtedly
unnecessary
until
usually

V
vacuum
varieties
vegetable
vengeance
vicinity

villain

W
Wednesday
weird
welfare

wherever
wholly
women
writing
written

SUMMARY OF PRACTICES FOR SPELLING MASTERY

1. By self-examination find the few words you misspell again and again. Make a list of them, and check it until you can recognize each troublemaker at a glance.
2. Correct the spelling fault of omitting, adding, and transposing letters in simple words by looking at the word. Many of the easiest words are misspelled because you have really never seen them.
3. Keep a handy list of the most confusing homonyms. Use it to avoid incorrect usage. Know the basic rules of spelling, and keep one or two examples in mind.
4. Keep your own list of spelling demons. Study the list of simple words most often misspelled. Compare your own list of troublesome words with other lists. Note your weaknesses by checking the type of mistake you make: is it the *ei—ie* word, is it the *ly* suffix, is it the dropped *e*? Locate your specific weakness and correct it. Conscious awareness is often more than half the remedy.

The final word on spelling is *vision.* There are so many exceptions to rule and sound in English that perhaps a sense of keen perception is the one best practice in becoming a proficient speller. People gifted with photographic minds, that is, with the visual-mindedness to recall what a page looks like, what is on it, etc., seem to be generally the best spellers. Then perhaps to *see critically* is to *succeed.*

WHY PUNCTUATE?

The function of punctuation is to "slow down" or "stop." The word *punctuation* comes from the Latin word *punctus,* meaning a point. Thus, the differently shaped points (marks) of punctuation keep words from running away. In the "slowing" and "stopping" process, marks of punctuation replace gesture, changes of voice, pauses, and changes of thought.

Punctuation usage has changed over the centuries. People used to read everything aloud, so punctuation maintained a closer control than is necessary for rapid, silent reading. As people learned to read silently, punctuation did not need to control as strictly. Modern writers use less punctuation than was the custom a hundred years ago. At the same time punctuation usage is flexible enough to be personal to a degree. Whether you use close or loose punctuation is not of first importance. Rather, you should know the basics of punctuation in order to convey your thoughts clearly to a reader. If you violate the rules, as sometimes you might for the sake of clarity or to avoid saying something barbaric, you should at least know that you are doing so.

THE CHARACTERISTICS OF THE MARKS OF PUNCTUATION

The character of the *period* is to indicate a full stop. It implies a pause at the end of a unit of thought standing alone.

Related to the period is the *semicolon,* whose nature is to indicate a "slowing down" between coordinate elements within a sentence—two clauses (related or parallel thoughts). The "slowing down" indicated by the semicolon may be compared to the slowing down of a car for the yellow traffic signal between the red and the green.

The *comma* is related to the semicolon in that it is a pause. However, it is much weaker, resembling in many respects a blinking caution light, which demands less "slowing down." *Parentheses* and the *dash* sometimes replace the comma in setting off added words or ideas (called parenthetical material). The writer is given certain freedoms in the use of each to achieve emphasis, variety, and to suit different conditions.

The nature of the *colon* is to indicate that something important is being introduced: (1) a significant explanation, (2) a long quotation, or (3) a list which may be words or groups of words.

One of the simplest of all the marks of punctuation is the apostrophe. It has three main uses: (1) to show *possession* (John, John's; somebody, somebody's; Caesar, Caesar's); (2) the *omission of letters* in words (doesn't, can't, won't, couldn't); and (3) the *plural* of letters or words when simply adding an *s* might cause confusion (k's, a's, too's, but's). Sometimes apostrophes are used for the plural of numbers (1960's, 6's).

With a knowledge of rules and an understanding of the nature of punctuation, you should have no difficulty choosing, where choice is allowed, to suit your own style of writing and distinctive conditions. In an essay entitled *Guide to Usage,* Harrison Platt, Jr., gives a wonderful bit of advice: "If a sentence is very difficult to punctuate," he writes, "so as to make the meaning clear, the chances are that the arrangement of words and ideas is at fault. The writer will do better if he rearranges his word order instead of wrestling with his punctuation."[3] This advice is worth remembering the next time you get bogged down in a stubborn sentence that won't say what you have in mind.

SUMMARY OF ENLIGHTENED PUNCTUATION

1. Appreciate the basic function of punctuation—to give your written word its final clarification.
2. Know the rules that govern the use of punctuation marks.
3. Know the nature and general character of the several punctuation marks, particularly those that perform related functions.
4. Use the freedom allowed the writer, within the rules, in order that punctuation may be personal and a part of the individual style in writing.
5. And remember always—if punctuation cannot clarify, change the word arrangement.

---

[3]Harrison Platt, Jr., "Guide to Usage, *The American College Dictionary* (New York: Random House, 1969), 1455.

LOOKING BACK

1. One of the suggestions for becoming a better speller is that you keep a list of the words you commonly misspell. What two additional suggestions for improving your spelling did you find in this chapter?

2.   THINK A-
                       HEAD

   Although the sign maker divided the word *ahead* properly into two syllables, the awkwardness of his message shows that he didn't think ahead. What advice could you have given him?

3. Most people remember the *ie, ei* rule by saying "*i* before *e*, except after *c*, or when as pronounced *ay*, as in neighbor or weigh."

   Make up a similar jingle for any of the other spelling rules in this chapter.

4. Insert the five punctuation marks referred to in this chapter (period, semicolon, colon, comma, apostrophe) where they belong in the following sentence:

   The store detectives boss gave him the following orders mingle with the crowds keep your eyes open for people with large bags be alert he promised he would do his best.

Chapter 8

Studying for Subjects: Developing a Feeling for Your Work

TRUE CONFESSIONS

1. The major subject areas in high school are English, social studies, mathematics, science, and foreign languages. Which of those areas give you the most trouble? Explain the reasons for your difficulty.

2. When Mrs. Green met her son's geometry teacher on Open-School Night, she was told that her boy had a defeatist attitude and expected to fail. Mrs. Green replied, "I'm not surprised he is doing poorly in your subject, because both my husband and I were weak math students in school."

   How should the teacher have responded to that comment?

3. Have you ever been asked by an adult, "What did you do in school today?" and answered, "Nothing"?

   Since it is obvious that you had done something, why did you answer that way? What makes a student bored with school? What would you think of young people who say that they are never bored in school?

4. What language, other than English, do you speak? Was it learned in the home or at school? It has been said that Americans are generally deficient in foreign language study. From your experience, is that true? If so, how can you explain it?

THE BEGINNING OF SUCCESS IS INTEREST

The word *educate* is closely related to the word *educe*. In the oldest pedagogic sense of the term, this meant drawing out of a person something potential or latent. We can, after all, learn only in relation to what we already know. Again, contrary to common misconceptions, this means that, if we don't know very much, our capability for learning is not very great.[1]

The desire to learn, to know, to become educated, comes from within. No one can learn for you, no one can become educated for you. When it comes to acquiring an interest in knowing, you are on your own. If you are lucky, you have a curious mind and a love of learning, and you probably think that school is a fairly decent place to be—better, say, than a bowling alley. On the other hand, if school bores you, perhaps you'd rather be bowling.

Nevertheless, as a student who someday might like to do more than knock down pins all day, your current responsibility is to *try* to become interested in your studies.

You can't necessarily expect to be interested in all assignments and all subjects, but have the courage to study the least interesting assignments first. Master a subject that does not appeal to you, and you will gain confidence in your ability to do difficult things. Developing interest in what you do requires an effort of will; with that effort drudgery will disappear to be replaced by appreciation and feeling.

---

[1] Neil Postman and Charles Weingartner, *Teaching as a Subversive Activity* (New York: Delta, 1969), 62.

RELISH FOREIGN LANGUAGES

The languages referred to here are those other than the one you grew up with. In our global village, we are only a few hours away from any part of the world, and successful study of another language can be of great advantage. Imagine yourself in a company seeking employees to be sent to a project in another country. The employees who get to go are those who have language qualifications. Will you be one sent or one left behind?

Speech, man's greatest invention, is the thing that makes us what we call "human" rather than "animal," the thing that provides a memory for mankind and the basis of all culture and civilization. This heritage is just as significant in Hebrew, Greek, Latin, French, German, Italian, Spanish, Chinese, and Japanese as it is in English. You can, therefore, approach the study of another language from the point of view that language study is one of the most broadening and cultural elements of your education.

You learned your first language slowly and with a great amount of repetition and practice. You used sounds over and over again—practice and more practice. In time, you could think in terms of words without having to say them out loud. As you learn a new language, practice, practice, and more practice is going to be a very important part of the program.

From rules of grammar you will learn how the words are arranged in sentences to impart meaning. You may learn to read some of the language and speak it before you learn the technical elements of grammar. You certainly did this with your first language. Learning the fundamentals of grammar is, perhaps, a sound way to start learning a second language, but other methods—using audio tapes, for example—may be equally effective. Many schools, including your own, may use a combination of teaching techniques to make the acquisition of a new language both pleasurable and worthwhile.

To Memorize: Write and Recite

➤Memorization is the key to learning vocabulary and the forms of various parts of speech, especially nouns, verbs, and adjectives. The first step in memorizing is to determine what it is that you need to learn. Certainly, your teacher will tell you precisely what you need to know.

➤The next step is for you to write down what you need to know in a form that is easy to use. For vocabulary building, try writing the words on cards, the word on one side, the English definition on the other; or write the words and their definitions in parallel columns on notebook paper, one column in the left margin and one in the right. (That way you will not be able to see both columns at the same time.)

For building your knowledge of forms, keep charts, such as the following.

For the present tense of the Spanish verb *ser*, meaning *to be*:

Person	Singular	Plural
1	soy	somos
2	eres	sois
3	es	son

In Latin, the noun meaning *leader:*

	Singular	Plural	
Nominative	dux	duces	Declension
Genitive	ducis	ducum	of third
Dative	duci	ducibus	declension
Accusative	ducem	dues	noun
Ablative	duce	ducibus	

➤ The third step in memory work is to recite *out loud* the whole stack of cards, list, or chart until you can recite them perfectly without looking. In the case of a list, start by breaking the list up into small groups, seven items to a group; learn the first group, then go on to the second. When you have learned the second, go back over the first and second together; then proceed to the third group, and so on, until you have learned the whole list or chart. Then put the list aside, and after eight to twenty-four hours, review the list *out loud,* again in the small groups, until you can recite the list perfectly once more without looking. The best time for such recitation and review may be immediately before going to bed—(It seems that your mind continues to review the list while you sleep!)—and upon awaking. The fourth step is once again to review orally the material to be learned within two days, and then within seven days. If you follow this procedure, the words may stay with you forever.

➤ Oral recitation also plays an important role in learning grammar. Make sure you understand *exactly* what the rules of grammar are that you are being asked to learn. Then as you study, recite them *out loud* until you have learned them. Make sure to use them. You will lose your knowledge of the rules if you don't use them. It may also help to compare and contrast the rules of grammar of a foreign language with the rules of grammar for English.

➤ Practice in hearing and speaking will develop your oral command of the language. Pay attention to your teachers, listen carefully to their pronunciation, and imitate their speech. Pay attention to your fellow students; as they recite, recite silently along with them, note their errors and the teachers' corrections.

➤ Reading and translating are two similar but distinct skills. Both require you to understand what a passage says and means. To translate, you must be able to write accurately in English what the passage says. To read, the student must understand, in the language itself, what a passage says. Fortunately, the same study techniques improve both skills. Read phrase by phrase rather than word by word, and guess at the vocabulary from context before looking up new words in a dictionary. Keep lists of words and idiomatic expressions you had to look up three or more times, and memorize them.

Hints for Language Study

1. Imitate fluent speakers as much as you can. Imitate your teacher and use your school's language lab.
2. Memorize vocabulary and forms until you know them and can recall them accurately, and study the grammar of English and the language you are learning.
3. Study *out loud* as much as you can.
4. Space your studying effectively. Break assignments up into small units, and review after every two or three units. Break your study time into periods of about twenty minutes. After each period, take a five-

minute break from hard studying, to review quickly or even to get up and move around a bit.

5. *Study every day.* When you are learning a foreign language, you are embarking on a journey through an unknown wilderness—your teacher is your guide, your text is your guide. Study every day, or you may lose your way.

ENGLISH GIVES MEANING TO FEELING

By now you must have noticed that this book emphasizes the importance of words and how important it is to learn and use them correctly and wisely. Reading and writing, after all, are the foundation of most learning. Words, and the beauty and power that can be coaxed from them, have made possible—for better or worse—the achievements and influence of figures like Lincoln, Lenin, Churchill, and Martin Luther King, Jr. Words can move us to tears and to action, and they give humankind the unique ability to express ideas and utter thoughts that have never been uttered before.

In your English courses, you are given the opportunity to develop your word power—as a reader, a writer, a speaker, and a listener. If your assignment requires that a sentence be written or spoken, make it the best sentence. If it is a course that requires reading a novel, story or poem, or listening to a speech or oral recitation, use your head, but give your heart a chance. This is the meaning of feeling.

> To follow knowledge like a sinking star
> Beyond the utmost bounds of human thought.[2]

---

[2]Alfred Lord Tennyson, "Ulysses," *Collected Poems* (London: Macmillan Co., 1842), 72.

Literature

In the study of English, you also will be asked to examine literature closely. Most of your time will be spent on fiction, but you also will read poetry, drama, essays, and, some non-fiction, such as biography and cultural history. As you read a work of literature, you will often be asked to know *what* the author has written, *how* the author has written it, and what *your response* has been to it.

As tools to express ideas about how authors write, your teachers and texts will use terms of literary criticism. Pay careful attention to terms such as *irony, tone, point of view, theme, plot, symbol,* and *figures of speech.* Make notes in your notebook explaining these kinds of terms and citing specific references to the work you are then reading. If you own the book you are reading, put notes in the margins.

Below are worksheets to use as you read different kinds of literature. Use them *before you read* to help your mind get set for reading critically, *while you read* to help you take notes, and *after you have read* to organize your review for tests.

WORKSHEET FOR A NOVEL

---

1. Who is the author? When and where did the author live? Knowing the historical and cultural context in which an author lived will help you understand the novel.
2. What is the title of the novel? Does it make you think of anything?
3. Who are the major and minor characters? Are they realistic? Why might the author not use realistic characters?

4. How does the author tell the story? For example, is the story told chronologically, in the third person, in the first person? Is the story one of action, or one of reflection, or of feelings? Does the author use foreshadowing or flashbacks?

5. Does the author use symbols or irony? Write down the recurrent symbols. Write down examples of irony, or at least note where they occur in the novel.

6. What is the setting of the novel? Where are the characters, what are they doing? Is the setting important to the story? Does the setting provide a framework for the story?

7. What is the theme of the novel? Can you write down in one sentence what message the author is trying to convey?

8. Does the author make any unusual use of language? Are the author's sentences short, simple, and direct; or are they long and full of subordinate clauses? Does the author use dialect? How effective is the author's style of sentences at conveying meaning?

WORKSHEET FOR A SHORT STORY

1. What is the title? As you read the title, does it bring to mind an image? Who is the author?

2. What is the setting and who are the characters? How well developed are the characterizations? Do the characters' names tell you anything about them?

3. What is the plot of the story? Everything depends on the storyline; without knowing it, you will lose track of other things.

4. Does the author create any abrupt contrasts such as light-dark, hot-cold, or contrasts of character? Does

the author use the contrast for dramatic effect or to convey extra meaning in brief form?

5. Does one of the characters tell the story? If so, how does that affect the story?

WORKSHEET FOR A PLAY

1. Who is the author? When and where did the author live?
2. Are there conventions of stagecraft particular to this author's era? How do these conventions limit what the author can do? Do the conventions affect the stage, scenery, actors, and characters?
3. What is the title? What does it tell you about the play?
4. What is the setting? What are the circumstances that have led up to the opening scene? (You probably will not be able to answer these questions until you have read the play.)
5. Is there a plot, is there action? Write down the story line briefly. (There may not be much action in some plays.)
6. Does the author use symbol, irony, metaphor, or other figures of speech? Are things as they appear on the surface, or is there deeper meaning underlying characters, actions, or scenes?
7. Can you classify the play as a tragedy or a comedy? How does the play fit into one or the other of these categories? If it is neither a tragedy nor a comedy, why does neither of these terms apply?
8. Can you write in a sentence what the play's theme is?

WORKSHEET FOR A POEM

1. Who is the author? When and where did the author live?
2. What is the title of the poem? Is it a fitting title? Does the title bring any image to mind?
3. Does the poem fit into a framework determined by rhyme and meter (for example, iambic pentameter) or determined by number of syllables (as in haiku)? Or is there no framework at all?
4. What does the poem tell you? Does it describe an emotion, a moment, or tell a story?
5. How does the author use language? Are there symbols, similes, metaphors? What images do the author's words convey? (Remember that poets try to convey their meaning in few words, and so even single words can convey great meaning.)

WORKSHEET FOR AN ESSAY

1. Who is the author? When and where did the author live?
2. What is the title of the essay? Is the title meaningful?
3. What is the author's thesis? What is the author arguing about or trying to prove?
4. Does the author use examples to illustrate the main points? What are some examples? Are the examples valid?
5. Does the author make an impassioned plea? How logical is the argument? Does the author make false assertions or denials?
6. Does the author argue successfully? Why is the author successful; or why does the author fail?

Expository Writing

Often in English class you will be asked to write essays on the literature you are reading or on a subject either assigned by the teacher or of your own choosing. As you write, you will be demonstrating what you know about the topic, the quality of your thinking, and your ability to write clearly, compellingly and correctly. In a sense, then, composing an essay is the culmination of your training in English.

For your essay writing to be forceful, you need to organize your thoughts carefully, present your arguments in a logical manner, and write sentences that are not only grammatical but also interesting to read. To organize your thoughts, create a brief outline, either on paper or in your mind, before writing; and as you create the outline, review the order of your ideas to check for effors in logical arrangement. To write sentences that are interesting to read, strive to pack several ideas into each sentence, and try to express repeated concepts in different words. Short, choppy sentences of one or two ideas and the use of the same words over and over again are the marks of an immature writer. Be on guard, however, against creating excessively long sentences; their very length may detract from their quality.

Just as most people follow a ritual when they get up in the morning, most writers adhere to a routine that helps them do their best work. Think about how you normally write an essay for school. Do you talk to others about the topic? Do you seek ideas or do they just come to you out of the blue? Do you preplan exactly what to say, or do you usually discover your point once the essay is underway? Before writing a draft, do you make notes or prepare an outline? Are you preoccupied with spelling and grammar as you write, or do you write freely? Do you reread as you go along or only at the end? How much do you actually write before revising anything? Do you habitually write in pencil, in pen, or on a computer?

Whatever your answers to these questions, you use some sort of process for writing essays. Through trial and error, you have probably found a process that works for you, but one that may change from time to time depending on the importance of the assignment and the amount of time you have to write it. Regardless of the details of your process, writing an essay generally comes in three stages. The first, *prewriting*, consists of all you do before you actually begin writing the text of your essay. During the second stage, *composing*, you choose words and form sentences that express your thoughts. And finally, during the *revising and proofreading* stage, you polish and refine the text of your essay word by word, making it true, clear, and graceful. Actually, the lines between the stages are not at all distinct, but in spite of blurry boundaries, it pays to keep the functions of each stage in mind.

Although every essay topic offers a different challenge, the basic principles of writing remain constant. Success in essay writing depends in large measure on how honestly you can respond *yes* to these twelve questions about good essay writing.[3] Use the questions as a checklist after you have composed your essay and before you turn in your final draft for a grade.

1. Have you studied the topic closely or answered the specific question being asked?
2. Have you narrowed the topic sufficiently to write about it within the permissible number of words?

[3] Adapted from George Ehrenhaft, *How to Prepare for SAT II: Writing* (Hauppauge, NY: Barron's, 1994), 170.

3. Have you clearly articulated the main point(s) you intended to make about the topic?
4. Have you collected ideas and arranged them in a sensible sequence?
5. Have you written an appealing and informative introduction?
6. Have you developed your ideas with specific examples and details?
7. Have you guided your readers with transitions between sentences and paragraphs?
8. Have you used plain, precise, lively, and fresh words?
9. Have you omitted needless words?
10. Have you varied your sentences to create interest?
11. Have you ended your essay unforgettably?
12. Have you followed the conventions of standard English and proofread your paper?

Usage and Grammar

In addition to the study of literature and to the development of your skills as a writer, you will study usage and grammar in English class. Although usage and grammar are often used interchangeably, usage describes the actual written and spoken language, and standard usage is that language used by educated people who occupy positions of leadership and influence in society. Grammar, on the other hand, is a set of rules, based on Latin, that describes or defines the way language is to be used. In your English class, you will probably receive some instruction in both usage and grammar. Like any complex system of rules, grammar takes time to master. Perseverance helps, but avoid getting bogged down trying to memorize every detail. Rather, save your energy for clearing up those problems in English usage that seem to recur in your speech and writing. When a paper is returned to you with a grade and a comment, it may often be marked up with various symbols that indicate errors. For example, your teacher may have pointed out a problem in agreement, or a faulty reference, or an incomplete sentence, or a comma splice. (Sometimes the number of possibilities for error seems infinite.) In order to correct the errors it helps considerably to know grammatical terminology. For instance, in the following sentence there is a problem with the agreement between subject and verb.

> <u>Delivery</u> (singular subject) of today's newspapers and magazines <u>have been</u> (plural verb) delayed.

Perhaps your ear will tell you that something is amiss in this sentence, but if not, you might easily figure out the problem if you knew the grammatical rule that subjects and verbs must agree in number and were familiar with the concepts of *subject, verb, singular*, and *plural.* It would help, too, if you knew that any noun that lies within a prepositional phrase (of today's newspapers and magazines) may never be the subject of a sentence.

The grammar textbook that you use in school may be of the traditional sort and use such terms as these, or it may not follow tradition and use terms different from these to describe what is going on in sentences. Regardless of the style, it will use terminology to name the functions of words and parts of sentences; and it may be in your best interest to know them.

One way to learn grammatical terms is to commit them to memory, just as you would memorize the parts of the human anatomy or an internal combustion engine. Unless you use the terms regularly, however, they're not apt to stick. Instead of memorizing, then, buy a good grammar book to keep by your side to consult as you would a dictionary or thesaurus. Whenever your papers are returned with errors marked, consult the book or arrange a writing conference with your teacher to discuss the problems. If the same errors recur on paper after paper, then it's time to approach the problem more diligently and systematically. In your notebook make lists of those errors, devise and study flashcards, ask your teacher for grammatical exercises. By paying close attention to the few errors you find yourself making consistently, you are certain to eliminate them from your writing. Concentrating on a handful of errors is a far more realistic approach than trying to grasp all the complexities of English grammar in one fell swoop.

HISTORY—ENJOY WHAT YOU CANNOT AVOID

A student who does poorly in history will often try to defend lack of interest by some such silly statement as "I am not interested in what is past, I am only interested in the present." If this sadly misdirected person could, by his own wishes, rid himself of history, he would "in the twinkling of an eye" reduce himself to the basic survival instinct and intellectual level of the lower animals.

Let us, using a case that seems within the realm of possibility, rid our person who has no interest in history from his contact with the past. Scientists are able to produce a gas capable of producing mass amnesia over a whole battlefront or city. Suppose enough of such a gas could be let loose to drift over the whole earth, following the prevailing winds over land and sea. Over the whole earth, progressively as the wind moved, history would be erased. The memory of the past, the total past, would be gone in an instant. The whole of mankind would be plunged abruptly into savagery. A person reading a book would stare blankly. Our friend who had no interest in the past, halfway home from school, would wander aimlessly, not remembering where she lived. She could meet others wandering with blank expressions, even her own parents, and neither would recognize the other. The point of the story is plain; if the past has no meaning, the present has no meaning, and there is no future.

So history for each of us is concerned with human knowledge and human need; and from the time when people first began to keep a record of events and things, they sensed the necessity to preserve the story for all who would come after them. The ancient historian Herodotus probably never asked what history was good for, but he thought of it as the ultimate form of entertainment. Thucydides, who came soon after, found in history a deeper and more useful good—lessons for the future from the incidents of the past. The patterns of the good of history have continued down through the centuries. "History makes men wise," said Francis Bacon. Supreme Court Justice Oliver Wendell Holmes, believing that history and intelligence are related, observed that "a page of history is worth a volume of logic." Many other people agree that it is nothing short of foolish to ignore history. As George Santayana put it, "Those who cannot remember the past are condemned to repeat it."

Each generation rewrites the history of the world in the light of new problems facing it, and its concern is ever with the human knowledge and the human necessity of each individual who comprises its generation.

Some students fail to get the most possible from history because they view it piecemeal. The results are an awareness of parts only—names, dates, events without relationships, and places without geographical or cultural implications; seeing, as it were, the trees without the forest. We need to look at history from a cycloramic point of view, supplemented by sufficient reflective power for the observers to see themselves; for it is only by seeing ourselves as a part of the whole story of universal history that meaning can become clear. It is commendable to know the date when Lincoln was born, and the exact moment when his heart stopped on that fateful April morning in 1865. But it is far more important to ponder why men of earth rise up and destroy the great among them. For if it is people who make people as they are—what have we made of ourselves?

Only when you have learned to think historically can you put yourself into history. Everyday experiences teach us that to get the most out of something, we must take an active part and become completely involved, to the extent that we feel that we are a part and "belong." Belonging leads to a feeling of relationship, which leads us to an appreciation of something larger than ourselves. Thinking historically helps us become more aware of a relationship that makes it possible for us to be more stable, to be more capable of accepting conditions beyond our immediate control, to seem more worthwhile to the world around us, and to find better reasons for our existence.

By thinking historically, you will recognize what facts are and be able to contrast them with statements of opinion. You will be able to organize facts clearly to write essays; and you will be able to assess your sources, judging whether they are eyewitness accounts (primary sources) or second-hand accounts (secondary sources). You also will be able to determine the bias of your source and judge the validity of the information it contains.

To succeed as a student of history you will need to pay particular attention to facts, for without them you will be unable to support your arguments in your essays. Use the *who, where, when, what*, and *why* method for remembering details of your history lesson. Put the person in the right place at the right time, know *what* was done and *why* it was done. The five w's make a complete picture; they bring the parts of the puzzle together.

For example: Early in World War II, Hitler, frustrated by his Luftwaffe's failure to subdue Britain from the air during the spring and autumn of 1940, turned east and invaded Russia in June of 1941, in violation of the Nazi–Soviet nonaggression pact he had signed with Stalin. In so doing, Hitler created a two-front war, a situation his generals had hoped to avoid. The five w's also make an outline through which the entire dramatic story of Hitler's fateful blunder will come back to you.

If you will practice the *who, where, when, what,* and *why* method for remembering your history lesson, you will find that many details, once lost, will remain with you. The five w's method of creating a complete picture of events is used by newspaper writers to present a clear story, and by lawyers to present clear and complete evidence to juries in court. Use it for studying your history lesson.

Hints for Studying History

1. Keep a list of important names, dates, events, and ideas in your notebook at the front of the section of notes.
2. Use a study method, as discussed in Chapter 5. History is the academic discipline best suited to the use of study methods.
3. Use a worksheet for dealing with your textbook. Use the sample work sheet that follows, or adapt it to your own needs.

WORKSHEET FOR TEXTBOOK ASSIGNMENTS IN HISTORY

---

1. What do I know about this assignment?
2. What can I find out about this assignment from a quick scan of the boldface type?
3. What do the study questions at the and of the chapter tell me about the assignment?
4. How does this assignment relate to previous assignments?
5. Read the assignments and take notes, using the $1/3$–$2/3$ format (See Chapter 6).
6. What topics of importance was I unable to predict in Part 2 and 3 above?
7. What are the important names, dates, in this assignment? *Remember the five w's—who, where, when, what, why.*
8. What questions will my teacher ask on tests about this assignment?

As part of your study of history, you may be asked to write research papers; and in doing the research for these, you will need to pay attention to the special demands the academic discipline of history places upon you. In addition to the regular requirements of research, you will need to weigh the validity of your sources. Primary sources are documents, letters, papers, speeches, and the like, that were written by people directly involved in the process or event you are investigating. These documents are eyewitness accounts, so to speak. Because they were written by people close to the origin of the event, these documents are to be considered of greater value than opinions written by men and women not directly involved. Newspaper or magazine articles, and books written by men and women who did not take part in the event are called secondary sources.

If, for example, you were doing a research paper on President Harry Truman's decision to drop the atomic bomb on Hiroshima and Nagasaki, primary sources would be notes, letters, and memoranda written by the president and his military, scientific, and political advisors. Secondary sources would include such works as *Danger and Survival* by McGeorge Bundy and *Truman*, a biography by David McCullough.

You may find it helpful to use worksheets in addition to your regular note-taking method when you are doing your research, so as to help you distinguish your primary sources from your secondary ones, and to weigh the importance of each source. Below are two worksheets.

WORKSHEET FOR PRIMARY SOURCES IN HISTORY

---

1. Who is the author of this document?
2. What do I know about the author?
3. When did the author write the document?

4. What sort of document is this? (Letter, speech, *etc.*)
5. For what purpose did the author write?
6. What can I expect to get out of this document?
7. What does this document say? (Write your notes according to the system you have already determined to use on notecards, for example.)
8. Does this document meet my expectations, as I expressed them above in my answer to Question 6? If not, why not?
9. What topics does this document encourage me to study in other sources or texts?

WORKSHEET FOR SECONDARY SOURCES IN HISTORY

---

1. Who is the author of this work? When did the author write this work?
2. Does this author present a balanced argument, or is his argument heavily weighted in one direction? If weighted in one direction, in which one?
3. For what purpose am I reading this work?
4. Make notes, according to the system you already have determined to use—on notecards, for example.
5. What other secondary sources does this work suggest I read?
6. What primary sources does this work suggest I read?

TRY SMILES INSTEAD OF FROWNS FOR MATHEMATICS

The ancient fascination and feeling for numbers have been passed down to us through the millenia. Centuries ago people sitting in a cave may have counted their fingers and discovered the number 10. And thus mathematics was born. If our ancestors had only four fingers, the structure of mathematics might be completely different. On the banks of the Euphrates River, about five thousand years ago, a people we call Sumerians assigned particular significance to the number 10, and today our decimal system is based on that all-important number.

The pages of history make it very clear that feeling for mathematics never slackened once numbers were discovered. The ancient Egyptians used a forty-inch measuring reed (called the *canon*) to lay out the Great Pyramid, which covers thirteen acres. The ancient Babylonians measured and laid out irrigation ditches and discovered geometry—the measuring of the earth. So this is mathematics, simple and mystic, practical and romantic, measuring the height of a newborn child in inches and the distance to a star in light years—one about twenty-one inches, the other 5,880 billion miles.

Mathematics can serve you profitably and give you much pleasure, or you can serve it as a resentful slave, waiting to finish the last required course. The basic step for you, as with all subjects, is to develop an interest in the intrinsic value of mathematics and in its importance to our lives.

To appreciate the value of mathematics, it is best to approach it as a way of looking at things, The poet sees the world in one light, the mathematician in another, and it follows that if you enjoy looking at things in literature through the eyes of the poet, you are capable of looking at things as seen through the eyes of the mathematician.

In addition to making the world around you more interesting, mathematics can serve you in the following ways.

➤ It can improve your ability to think clearly and precisely. Although there is a great deal of memorization and recall in the study of mathematics, there is also the application of knowledge, the applying of old patterns to new things, calling on you to use your hunch or best guess to find a new relationship that was not anticipated when you began a problem.

➤ The study of mathematics can improve your powers of observation. No reading requires keener observation of exactly what is written and precisely what is being asked.

➤ The study of mathematics and its history can provide an appreciation for the marvelous workings of the mind of man. We could learn how some 2,200 years ago, Eratosthenes, with a deep well in Syrene, Upper Egypt and a post hole at Alexandria, 574 miles away, and an angle of $70°\ 12''$ to the sun, calculated the circumference of the earth to be 24,662 miles—missing by only 195 miles, or an error of less than one percent. Or we could study Euclid, whose geometry was used longer than any other work except for the Bible; or Archimedes, perhaps one of the half-dozen greatest thinkers who ever lived. Or we could study the work of earth's space scientists, who, with the aid of computers, can determine the exact moment when a speeding asteroid will crash headlong onto the surface of the planet Jupiter, millions of miles away.

But our feeling for arithmetic, algebra, or geometry cannot long survive based only on the history of mathematics. A practical approach is necessary—a study of our own skills and an understanding of the language of mathematics.

There are tests available in the basic skills—handling of decimals, word problems—that can be used to identify areas of weakness. Such tests include SAT I and the ACT, samples of which are available in bookstores everywhere. Your math teacher may also be able to give you drills, exercises, and tests. You also could keep track of the mistakes you make on homework papers. Once you have identified trouble areas, you can take sensible steps to be aware of your problems and check your work on them carefully.

A real feeling for mathematics will develop with understanding of words and definitions. Although the scope of mathematics has increased more in the past fifty years than it did in twenty-two centuries from Euclid to Einstein, the vocabulary has grown even faster. The old words—addition and multiplication—are still in use, but new words and phrases—transformations, imaginary numbers, spreadsheets, composition, quantifiers, matrices—are now appearing in math books. You will need to use the definitions found in the particular book you are studying, so the index should be used as a guide to review basic words until you know them.

There are several things you also can do to enhance your performance in mathematics classes.

➤ Take note of the format of the textbooks you use. These books may have visual aids to help you identify significant ideas: different colors of print, shaded areas, or boxes. Your textbooks also will have sample problems, with all the steps included, in order to show you the necessary steps in the correct process of reaching an answer. And, of course, there will be many problems for you to solve by using the procedures illustrated by the sample problems. In many recent textbooks there is an answer key at the back so that you may check your work for accuracy.

➤ Pay close attention in class to what your teacher is saying and doing, and make careful notes. (Be sure to label your paper as class notes, and be sure to put the date at the top.) Copy down the problems your teacher solves on the board, since they will probably be problems containing the essence of the topic under discussion. (These problems may also be typical of problems you will find on quizzes and tests.) Do not take these class notes on your homework papers. If you do, you will confuse what you have done at home with what you have done in class, and there might be errors on your homework paper that will confuse you as you study from the notes later.

➤ As soon as you can after math class, neatly rewrite the notes you took in class that day, separating the important material from the scratch work. Then review your notes regularly. You will also gain ground if you rework the problems your teacher put on the board during class. If you cannot do these soon after class, at least make sure to rework them before beginning your homework. By solving these problems again, you will be reinforcing all the knowledge you have gained from that day's class.

➤ Try to be as neat as you can when taking notes in class, when completing assignments, and when taking tests. Write your symbols clearly and large enough to be read easily, and make sure that the problems are clearly separated from one another on the page. Also, try to be complete, showing the work you have done to reach the answer. Finally, when you are doing homework, leave space for your corrections, so that if your solution is wrong, you can correct the error on the page.

➤ Read your text carefully; read with paper and pencil in hand; and as you read, notice the visual aids in the text and what they are highlighting. When you come across a sample problem, cover the solution with paper and solve the problem yourself. Then check your solution with the one in the text to make sure that you have the correct answer and that you have included all the proper steps.

➤ Do all homework assignments only after reading your text, solving the sample problems correctly, and reviewing your notes from class. You can never review enough. After you have solved an assigned problem, compare your answer with the one in the answer key at the back of the textbook. If your answer is incorrect, solve the problem again, and compare your answer again. If you still are incorrect, put a star beside the problem on your homework paper, and ask your teacher about that problem at the start of your next class.

➤ Perhaps most important of all, keep all old quizzes and tests. Quizzes will show what your teacher thinks is important and will identify typical problems. Use these quizzes as guides for studying for tests, and solve the problems on them again as part of your studying for tests. Because tests on a chapter of the textbook will identify problems of major significance, you will benefit if you use them as study guides for unit tests and exams. As with quizzes, solve the problems again as part of your studying.

➤ Finally, practice doing math on a calculator. Chances
are that you already have a calculator of your own or
that your school will loan one to you. The calculator is
literally eliminating many of the mathematical operations that students formerly spent months learning,
such as using logarithms, finding standard deviations,
and calculating maximums and minimums. Mastering
the functions of a calculator will save you lots of time
and trouble, and who knows, may improve your grades
and change your entire outlook on math.

Along with calculators, computers are changing the
face of mathematics instruction. If you have access to
a computer at home or at school, take advantage of the
riches it offers. Even if computer instruction is not
part of your school's curriculum, you can teach yourself how to use spreadsheets and graphing programs.
Computers will give you new insights into organizing
and visualizing mathematical problems and information, not to mention new and attractive ways to present
solutions.

Although calculators and computers are marvelous
tools, they can't do the learning for you. Don't be
lulled into complacency by their power and incredible
speed. As tools of learning they are indispensible, but
they can't take the place of the human brain—not yet,
at any rate.

STUDYING SCIENCE

Your own science course in school—whether general
science, earth science, biology, chemistry, or physics—
can deepen your appreciation of the world in which
you live and add new dimensions to that world. The
study of science will demand an exactness in reasoning, a precision in observation, and a thoroughness in

execution similar to those required of you in mathematics; for, of course, mathematics is the tool of science.

Common to all scientific studies is a method of inquiry, usually called the scientific method. The scientific method has three basic parts: *the creation of hypotheses, the collection of data by experimentation,* and *an analysis to test the validity of the hypotheses.* These parts need not come in the order given, but for any scientific inquiry to be complete, the scientist must perform all three parts.

There are some things you can do in science class to improve the quality of your studying, things that are useful in any of the sciences.

➤ Make a quick survey of the chapters of your textbook. Is there a preliminary paragraph in the chapters that tells you what you will be learning? Are important terms printed in boldface type or in italics? Are units of the chapters numbered? Are there study questions at the end of the chapters, or perhaps summaries or review outlines? Are there visual aids to help signal important information (such things as boxes, shaded areas, different colors of print)?

➤ Look at the back of the textbook for a glossary and an index. The glossary will be helpful when you are learning new technical terms, the index will help you find a topic easily when you are reviewing. Check also for appendices. Many textbooks have several kinds of charts, lists of important scientific laws, formulas, and other types of important information in sections at the back of the book. Check also for an answer key if your textbook contains problems to solve. You will be able to check your answers for accuracy if there is an answer key.

➤ Make sure to follow all instructions carefully when you are doing laboratory work. Take careful notes in a laboratory notebook, and make sure not to mingle your lab notes with the notes you take in class or from your textbook. Make sure to write clearly in your lab notebook and to take down all the necessary information. Illegible notes and incomplete lab notes will prevent you from having the information necessary to complete your report of the experiment.

There are also some things to do when preparing for science class that are fairly specific to the science being studied.

General Science, Physical Science, or Earth Science

Follow all procedures carefully, since it is likely that in your beginning science course you will be introduced to laboratory work. Also, pay close attention to the scientific method, and make sure that you understand it and how to perform all three functions.

Biology

1. Learn how biological scientists have classified information about living things and what is the reasoning process that is the basis for the classification system. You may be required to memorize some of this system, and your understanding of how the system works will make this task easier.
2. In a special section of your notebook, make a list of the biological terms you need to know. This list may become very long and may be a very important part of your notebook, for important terms in biology are perhaps more numerous than in other sciences.

3. Pay close attention to the details of the drawings that your teacher puts on the board and that are in your textbook. Make sure that the drawings you put in your notes are both accurate and clear.

Chemistry

1. Recognize that it is very important to know and to understand the procedures to be used in chemistry. Learn *why* you are following a certain procedure, since merely memorizing the steps in a procedure will not usually give you sufficient knowledge to adapt it to new situations or experiments.

2. Most of the work you do in problem solving in the first year of your study of chemistry will call upon an understanding of many of the procedures you learned in algebra. Be ready to apply what you have learned in algebra to your problem solving in chemistry. If you haven't studied algebra already when you begin chemistry, take heart, you will be able to keep up in class if you work hard to understand and apply the procedures used in problem solving as they are explained in your textbook or by your teacher. Also, many chemistry textbooks contain an appendix devoted to the mathematics necessary in chemistry. If you need extra help with the mathematics, look for such an appendix, or ask your teacher for extra help.

3. When reading your textbook, have paper and pencil in hand so that you can take notes and work out the equations given in the text.

Physics

1. As in chemistry, in physics it is necessary for you to understand why you are using procedures and

performing operations. Mere memorization of steps will usually not be sufficient.

2. Also as in chemistry, in the first year of physics you will be able to use the knowledge you have gained of algebra. Be ready to transfer your learning to a new subject.

3. In class write the problems your teacher puts on the board clearly in your notebook, making sure to label them as class notes. It is likely these problems will be similar to the problems you will see on tests.

4. As you read your assignments, do so with paper and pencil, and practice working out problems and equations. As much as you can, practice solving problems and working out equations. Such efforts are never wasted.

LOOKING BACK

1. Let us assume that you are tutoring a friend having trouble in biology. What plan might you develop in order to help?

2. What does the quotation "No mathematician can be a complete mathematician unless he is also something of a poet" mean to you? What possible relationship is there between mathematics and poetry?

3. While this chapter has different approaches for helping you to study more effectively in the major subject areas, there are some suggestions that are common to all subjects. Can you name three of them?

4. The first part of the scientific method is the creation of hypotheses. What are the other two parts?

Chapter 9

Reading: Faster With More Understanding

TRUE CONFESSIONS

1. I'm a fast reader, all right," Sarah said. "The only trouble is that I can't remember what I read."

   Is Sarah's problem your problem? Have you ever "read" an entire page or chapter in a book without being able to remember any of the material you just covered? Is there an easy cure for this common experience?

2. Ellis said, "I can generally remember names because of my system of connections. For example, when I'm introduced to someone named Harry Butler, I think of a hairy servant. Rose Graves was easy—a red flower on a tombstone. But I'm having difficulty with Feodor Dostoyevsky!"

   What system, if any, do you use to remember names?

3. Generally, we read different material in different ways. For example, you might approach your chemistry book with more determination than you would read the television listings.

   On a scale of 1–10 (10 being the highest level of concentration), how closely would you typically read each of the following?

A poem you found in a magazine _____
The sports page of your school newspaper _____
A novel for English class _____
A chapter on reading faster and with greater
understanding _____
Directions for using a Walkman _____
The back of a cereal box _____
Information on how to enter the sweepstakes _____

THE NATURE OF READING

"Reading is to the mind what exercise is to the body,"
said the eighteenth-century essayist Joseph Addison,
and echoed by designer Calvin Klein in his late
twentieth-century TV commercials. Unless we enrich
our own thoughts by the great legacy of thought put in
books for us, our minds miss the exercise needed for
development, and perform with no greater measure of
efficiency than the athlete who has neither trained nor
practiced. As knowledge of words improves reading, so
reading improves knowledge of words; for words are
the tools of thinking, and reading is the storehouse
from which comes most of our thinking.

The three objectives of a good reader are: (1) to
concentrate on what is being read, (2) to remember as
much as possible, (3) to apply or associate what is read
to one's own experience. The three general types of
reading are (1) *Skimming*—this is quick scanning to
find a particular fact (when Alexander the Great died or
what follows John F. Kennedy's "ask what you can do
for your country" phrase). Skimming may also be rapid
reading for the main idea without bothering to gather
accompanying details. (2) *Careful Reading*—this is
reading that directs itself toward finding the main
topics, fixing them in mind, judging what the important

details are, and relating them to the main topics. (3) *Intensive Reading*—this is reading that directs itself to mastery of technical material, instructions in textbooks and on tests, textbook information that is cumulative, these requiring intensive reading that demands total understanding.

These types refer chiefly to work-type reading rather than reading for pleasure, although it is questionable whether anyone having a desire to learn does not always read with a great degree of pleasure. All practices for the development of better reading deal in one way or another with three aspects: (1) what to look for, (2) how to improve comprehension, (3) how to increase speed. As in methods of studying an assignment, it soon becomes apparent that different practices for improvement are generally variations rather than separate approaches. After you have seen the suggestions for improving the three areas noted above, perhaps you will then choose and modify according to your individual needs. Perhaps you can make new methods that will serve you better. If you are like the great majority of readers, your first and most difficult task will be to convince yourself that you can improve your reading habits.

By the time you finished elementary school you might well have said, "I know how to read," but research has shown that even the most literate and educated adults can always learn to read better. Moreover, the pages of literature are filled with testimony that bears witness to the diligence in both practice and time if one is to constantly improve one's reading ability. Listen to Johann Wolfgang von Goethe, poet, novelist, and philosopher, "The dear good people don't know how long it takes to learn to read. I've been at it eighty years, and can't say yet that I've reached the goal."

Henry David Thoreau, in his classic, *Walden,* or *Life in the Woods,* includes an essay on reading. Indeed, the whole of *Walden,* would be an excellent practice field for the three areas of improvement, Thoreau says of reading (the italics are the author's):

> To read well—that is, to read true books in a true spirit—is a *noble exercise,* and one that will *task the reader more than any exercise* which the customs of the day esteem. *It* requires *training* such as the *athletes underwent,* the *steady intention almost* of the *whole life* to this object. *Books must be read as deliberately and reservedly as they* were *written.*[1]

Continuing in the same essay, he writes:

> Most men have learned to read to serve a paltry convenience, as they have learned to cipher (count) in order to keep accounts and not be cheated in trade; but *of reading as a noble intellectual exercise they know little or nothing, yet this only is reading in a high sense,* not that which lulls as a luxury and suffers the nobler faculties to sleep the while, but *what we have to stand* on top-toe to read and *devote our most alert* and *wakeful* hours to.[2]

Reading for Understanding

How well do you understand what you read? Do you understand everything, or are you like many students who, when faced with pages of unfamiliar material, flee from the task by tossing the book aside. Or have you

---

[1]Henry David Thoreau, *Walden*, or *Life in the Woods* (New York: The Heritage Press, 1939), 110.
[2]Ibid., 110.

developed all sorts of ingenious techniques to avoid reading altogether? Do you say that you are too tired or that you have a headache? Do you pretend to read but sit there and daydream instead? Many people avoid reading because they don't feel confident of their ability, yet they are too proud to admit that fact. Others avoid reading because they don't remember enough of what they read; to them, reading seems like a waste of time. Some readers begin reading a story or a newspaper but quickly lose interest.

Sometimes a reading problem is a matter of eye-sight, solved for a few dollars by buying a pair of reading glasses. Sometimes, of course, the problem may be more serious. Recognizing that you have a reading problem, however slight, is the first step in solving it. The fact that you are reading this book, however, suggests that (1) you want to be a better reader, and (2) the measures for improved reading described in this chapter can help you to become one.

A crucial practice for improving your reading is to get into the habit of thinking about what you read, talking to other people about it, and comparing your thoughts with theirs. Of course, if you find the reading material dull, silly, or pretentious, there's not much to think or talk about. That's why your very first task is to get your hands on material that will grab your interest. What interests you? If you have a hard time answering that question, stop at the library and walk around for half an hour looking at books and magazines. The variety is remarkable, and, unless your brain is more dead than alive, you will surely find something to engage you, something that can be integrated into your life.

What to Look For

As you begin to improve your reading ability, practice looking for ideas in what you read. Yes, all reading material consists of individual words, but you should train yourself to look for ideas and thoughts rather than at words. Words are merely the symbols and labels used to portray the thoughts of the author. The reader does not take the words from the printed page; they remain. What the reader takes from the page are ideas and thoughts (idea is used here to designate a portion of a thought); consequently, they are what you should train yourself to find. Mere word reading hinders this process of finding ideas. Perhaps the best way to rid one's self of word-reading is to begin all reading by getting a quick bird's-eye-view.

Turn back to the passages by Thoreau. Do not plod from word to word. Skim rapidly over the passages and try to pick up from the italicized sections the main thought: *Reading is a noble intellectual exercise, requiring more training than most people are willing to devote to it.* Now go back and enjoy reading the entire passage. The facts will not become jumbled and confusing, and the organization and purpose will stand out clearly.

Since it is plain that the best way to obtain a bird's-eye-view is to find quickly the core of the paragraph, then each paragraph indentation should alert the reader. The quick motion of going over the paragraph for the central thought removes the stagnant, almost motionless operation of the word-reader, creeping up on a word, or as it sometimes seems, waiting for the word to crawl to the reader. A second result of this practice is to give the reader an awareness of thoughts. This may be compared to looking at the forest first and then approaching to look at the trees. The return to pick out the contributing ideas from the sentences that make up the paragraph is comparable to looking at the trees, but no one looks at every tree in the forest—only significant ones are observed. Perhaps this procedure could be best remembered by the formula:

$$P + S = CT$$
Paragraph + Sentence = Complete Thought

A formula for what to look for in reading without a *W* to stand for *words*—how strange! You will, of course, see words, but only as necessary labels for ideas. They will no longer be the purpose for which you are reading.

Knowing what to look for in reading presupposes a basic knowledge of paragraph patterns and sentence structure. What a paragraph is, quick recognition of how it is developed, ability to focus in on the topic sentence, getting the idea label from sentences—these are the things the reader must look for and see instantly. The four basic types of paragraphs are *exposition, description, narration,* and *argumentation.* These basic forms of discourse may be put in various patterns of paragraphs: (1) question and answer, (2) comparison and contrast, (3) cause and effect, (4) opinion and proof, (5) repetition of example, and (6) multiplication of details. One or two examples will show you how quickly comprehension follows if you know exactly what you are looking for.

Here is a question-and-answer paragraph (the italics are the author's):

How should you read? As you please. If you please yourself by reading fast, read fast; if you read slowly and do not feel like reading faster, read slowly. Pascal does not say we are apt to read too fast or too slowly, but he blames only an excess.

Montaigne complains of a formal way of reading. "My thoughts go to sleep when they are seated," he says, "so they and I walk." Honest industry merely jogs along, curiosity flies on Mercury's pinions. Passionate reading not only flies, it skips, but it does so only because it can choose, which is a high intellectual achievement. How do you read the timetable? You skip till you come to your place; then you are indifferent to the whole world and engrossed by your train, its departure, arrival, and connections. The same thing with any formula for the production of the philosopher's stone.

Whatever we read from *intense curiosity* gives us the *model of how we should always read. Plodding along page after page* with an equal attention to each word *results in attention to mere words. Attention* to *words never produces thought,* but very promptly results in distractions, so that an honorable effort is brought to nought by its own ill-advised conscientiousness.[3]

But suppose for a moment the reader reads the initial question without seeing it, and this is quite possible for the word-reader. If such be the case, the whole paragraph is lost, because there can be no answer unless there is a question.

Note the essentials of the topic sentence in this ex-pository paragraph (again the italics are the author's):

---

[3] Ernest Dimnet, *The Art of Thinking* (New York: Simon and Schuster, Inc., 1928).

Among the many kinds of material we must find in books, at least *three* are readily distinguished: *happenings, facts and principles.* Happenings—the narratives of *what* has *occurred*—concern us in *all forms of fiction,* whether as plays, novels, or stories. And *happenings* are a major part of all *history* and *biography.* Throughout such narratives and in almost all *sorts of writing* we encounter *facts* that may lack narrative connection: dates, names, locations, definitions, descriptions of processes. Less concrete than either happenings or facts, and often *harder* to *remember,* are *principles:* the *translation* of *facts into* statements of *law,* the *interpretation* of *happenings* as *cause* and *effect, or* the attempts to explain *human experience* in the *form* of *theories.*[4]

The topic sentence is made to alert the reader; the signal word *three* gives the clue. The body of the paragraph explains what *happenings, facts,* and *principles* are. The reader who knows what to look for will not have to reread this paragraph.

Here is a summary paragraph for this part of the chapter. Will it help you remember what to look for in your reading?

Summary Paragraph

What does the good reader look for? First, for the only thing that can be gleaned from the printed page, thoughts. Second, the reader looks for action on a wide screen—moving quickly over the page, getting a bird's-eye-view. Third, a good reader knows the form of discourse, patterns of paragraphs, and structure of

---

[4]E. Wayne Marjarum, *How to Use a Book* (New Brunswick: Rutgers Univ. Press, 1947), 4.

sentences so thoroughly that they add to the action of reading by almost literally jumping from the page to meet the reader. Finally, the reader looks with an eye to selection and classification of the kinds of material found in books—happenings, facts, and principles. What all good readers look for in their reading causes them to think, and indeed, all effective reading is thinking.

UNDERSTANDING MORE

The second major area that concerns the reader who wishes to improve (and doubtless few of us are ever far from this problem) is how to comprehend more of what we read and remember it longer.

The first step toward greater comprehension and longer retention is *purpose*—a clear realization of the objectives to be attained by manner and subject. Skillful readers aim to coordinate their purpose with the purpose of the writer, thinking with, and pursuing the same goals that the author had in writing. In an essay titled *A Teacher Looks at Reading,* A. B. Herr classifies the purposes of writers under three major divisions:

> (1) to give information—an intellectual opera-
> tion; (2) to share experiences, sentiments, and
> convictions—an operation which includes intellec-
> tual comprehension but is not complete without
> emotion, the feeling of having participated; and
> (3) to persuade, to change options, responses, or
> habits—an operation whose success depends on
> emotional acceptance, no matter how intellectual
> the approach may appear.[5]

[5] A. B. Herr, "A Teacher Looks at Reading," Alfred Steppernd, ed., *The Wonderful World of Books: Collection of Essays* (Boston: Houghton Mifflin Co., 1953), 83.

The nature of the assignment for work-type material will generally dictate the purpose. Once the purpose has been established the reader will then decide which of the three types of reading will be best: (1) skimming, (2) careful, or (3) intensive, or a combination. If the purpose is to locate information, skimming will suffice; but mastery that demands gathering facts and understanding their interrelationship, forming opinions backed by substantial evidence, might well dictate skimming first—followed by careful or intensive reading.

A second practice for better comprehension and easier retention is to condition the mind for positive rather than negative results. Many readers, faced with a difficult passage or assignment, start by expecting *not* to be able to understand and remember. This prepares the mind psychologically for defeat. Expect to understand and remember, and for a while it is excellent training to speak aloud to one's self: "I am going to remember this after one reading." Would the runner win the race if at the starting gun he said to himself, "I know I can't win"? Would high jumpers clear the bars if they said just before they left the ground, "I know I won't clear it"? Purpose plus confidence will, with the reader's help, interact to insure comprehension and retention.

A third aid to comprehension and retention is to read with questions in mind. The right questions can result in helping the readers enclose what they are reading with experience or association, thus making information so personal as to make forgetting impossible. What would you have done at the Battle of Thermopylae? Would you have enjoyed walking and talking with Milton as he felt his way along his garden path with his cane? Could the author have stated this rule more clearly? The example seems rather vague, what could I use as a better one? "There is no such thing as an interesting book or assignment"; to paraphrase Emerson, "there are only interested readers." And it might be added that only interesting questions make interested readers. How is this assignment related to the preceding one? Will what I already know about the topic make it easier for me to remember the facts I am now adding? And when a section or chapter is finished, self-recitation questions about main topics and how successfully, or unsuccessfully, the author has presented them will increase your ability to remember more of what you have read.

Retaining what is read is aided by finding some unifying association or significance. Facts and ideas can be very dull, but if some relationship can be established, whether logically or arbitrarily, it can serve as a packaging device and function as a convenient package.

Remembering Longer

Into much of the reading done in school must be introduced the learning skill that always causes students to shudder—memorization. It need not be an awesome word, and you need not fear it. Perhaps you would have a clearer understanding of much that you have to read if your teacher did not try to avoid using it by substituting phrases such as "learn all" or "learn each of the ten rules."

The first step in improving your powers of memory and putting them to work in your reading is to find out the kinds of ideas you remember with less difficulty than others—whether happenings, facts, or principles, and the element in each that helps you remember.

Some people remember color, others motion, still others cannot remember numbers when they are spelled out. General U. S. Grant could not remember the names of three consecutive towns he passed while marching, but on a topographical map he could memorize dozens of towns and their location in a matter of seconds. Alexander the Great could not remember the names of some of his close acquaintances, but he could memorize poetry with almost no effort.

Psychologists are generally agreed that each of us has not one memory power but many. By testing whether it is faces, places, dates, designs, pictures from reality, pictures from imagination, association with the physical or mental world that we remember more easily, we can find our memory strengths and use them as the association frames upon which to hang what is to be remembered.

One very simple but effective test is to think quickly of a boy (or a girl) you met recently. How do you remember him? By what he was doing? By the place where you saw him first? By who was with him? By the color of his shirt or jacket? By some number— books he was carrying, steps forward to shake hands, words spoken? By what he really looked like?— (reality). By what you thought he might have looked like?—(imagination). Which do you remember more distinctly—his handshake? (physical)—or what he said? (mental). Apply the same test to a character you meet in your reading.

When association and memory are not sufficient because the facts to be remembered are so numerous, the reader's last recourse is to take notes. If you own the book you are reading, marginal notes and the designation of important points by some system of marking suited to your purpose and kept consistent can be invaluable.

One of the simplest methods of designating degrees of importance is to use one, two, or three vertical lines: I for important, II for very important, and III for must remember. Some students use a (?) question mark to indicate further study needed; some use T or Ex. to signal likely test or examination material. One splendid practice for marginal notes is to write the paragraph main thought of a paragraph in a brief question beside the pararagraph. Some students try to summarize with such brevity as to include the summary at the end of each paragraph.

Note-taking on what you read forces you to think and to be constantly alert for the essentials. Such notes can be kept in better order and made available for quick use if taken on 3 × 5 index cards. These can he filed by subject or book for any desired reference or project, and are far more easily arranged than pages of a looseleaf notebook or binder.

A review of summary writing and outlining will afford you two methods of taking notes on what you read. There are, however, two additional types of reading notes sometimes used: (1) question and answer and (2) word and phrase list. The question-and-answer method states the question in full and then gives key words or phrases to indicate the answer. For example:

I. What does a good summary contain?
   A. Principal ideas
   B. Author's point of view
   C. Student's vocabulary

II. What are the steps in making a summary?

   A.

   B.

   C.

The question and answer method sharpens your attentiveness and enforces the questioning attitude. Once practiced it leads to clear-cut distinctions between major and minor topics.

The word-and-phrase-list form of notes on reading is little more than an unorganized outline. It is used most often for immediate use, such as reviewing quickly for tests. It offers a series of warning signals, reminding the reader what to remember. For example, this chapter might be summarized as follows:

READING: FASTER WITH MORE UNDERSTANDING

LOOK FOR
Bird's-eye-view
Thoughts
Main topics

COMPREHENSION
Writer's aim
Questions on material
Happenings
Facts
Principles

RETENTION
Memory powers
Application and
   association
Marginal notes
Written notes

INCREASING SPEED
Self-tests
Conscious purpose
Hollow triangle
Mechanics
Cautions

Note that words indicating principal parts are in italics. The student may find it useful to use *SUMMARY, OUTLINE,* or *QUESTION AND ANSWER,* except for more informal and less demanding subject matter.

READING FASTER

The third principal area for improvement in reading has to do with the speed at which you read. It is an established fact that fast readers are more accurate and remember more than slow readers. And, of course, they have the great advantage of saving much time. Slow readers lose their train of thought, and often their place on the page, among words; whereas fast readers read several words at a glance and are consequently dealing only in thoughts. There are many self-tests available for measuring your reading speed and comprehension. Your English teacher may be able to provide you one, or perhaps even administer such a test. This should be your first operation. Find out how fast you read at present, and how much you comprehend of what you read. If you have reading difficulties, the test will probably pinpoint areas where specific practices can help.

How do we read? First of all, every reader faces the problem of coordinating the mind and the eye. The mind is capable of receiving ideas much more rapidly than the eye is able to receive and relay them. Thus, the problem of mind-wandering arises. If we do not discipline the mind to remain ready, it escapes to thoughts of ourselves, friends, what we are going to do later—and suddenly we have lost our place on the page. The slower one reads the more difficult it is to control the mind; therefore, rapid reading is training the eye to speed up and the mind to accept the eye's pace.

Our eyes move across the page by a series of quick stops, not in a flowing, even movement. These stops are called fixations, and whether we see one word or several at a fixation determines our speed of reading. Fast readers, who will always remember more of what they read than slow readers, make two or three fixations as they read the line of print, and they see groups of words, ideas, and thoughts. Slow readers are usually addicted to interrupting the forward movement across the page to glance backward. This is called "regression" and is a bad and confusing habit resulting from reading without sufficient purpose and speed. Good readers sweep from the end of the finished line downward and to the beginning of the next with no difficulty; slow readers will often make two or three false starts on beginning a line, and frequently reread the line just read or skip the one they should read. This, of course, is not completely the fault of the eye. Until the eye and the brain are working together, all these sloppy and fatal habits of reading prevail. Mechanical practices will help, but the determined effort to concentrate on increasing speed and comprehension, and a willingness to make each assignment a practice in better reading habits, will prove a great aid.

One mechanical aid to measure your "recognition span," the number of words you see at a fixation, may, however, be recommended. From an index card or some other semi-stiff material cut out a hollow triangle. Make the base wide enough to take in six or eight words. Place it on the line and move from top to bottom to determine how many words you see at a fixation. It may be used for a few minutes' practice each day, or as a test from time to time to measure improvement. Progress may also be noted on a chart on which you can enter the number of pages (of similar type material) that you can read in a 15-minute period. If you are putting serious effort into reading improvement this test might be done weekly.

Careful self-analysis of your own capacities will dictate your methods. Be cautious about developing speed with comprehension. Nervous haste without understanding will produce no beneficial results. Let the purpose determine the speed. Concentrate on correcting the obvious faults of the slow reader, and the increase in speed will usually take care of itself.

Above all else, keep three things in mind. One, that most study problems have as their basis a reading problem. Two, improvement in reading is a lifetime process. Three, if we read, we can become better readers; if we do not read, we become increasingly poorer readers.

PRACTICES FOR BETTER READING

➤ Prepare the mind psychologically for positive results.

➤ Know the three aims of a good reader:
  – to concentrate on what is being read,
  – to remember as much as possible, and
  – to apply or associate what is read to one's own experience.

➤ Know the three general types of reading and the type of material to which each may be profitably applied:
  – skimming,
  – careful reading, and
  – intensive reading.

➤ Know that the good reader looks for:
  – thoughts,
  – bird's-eye-view,
  – main topics, and
  – pattern and structure in picturing ideas.

➤ Understand the approaches to better comprehension and retention:
- — Reading is a conversation with the author.
- — Remember the purpose for which the reader is reading.
- — Always read with questions in mind.
- — Use memory powers to improve retention by association and application.
- — Make use of written notes.

➤ Make a determined effort to increase speed of reading:
- — Use self-tests for speed and rate of improvement.
- — Know the mechanical functions of the eye in reading.
- — Keep in mind the faults of the slow reader.
- — Know that fast readers remember more of what they read than slow readers.
- — Discipline the eye to take in more at a fixation.
- — Remember that speed without understanding is useless.

LOOKING BACK

1. Why is so much emphasis being placed on speed in reading? If students can absorb the material only by reading at a snail's pace, should they be concerned about reading faster? Why?

2. The acronym to help you remember the four basic types of paragraphs is EDNA: identify the four types and describe them briefly.

3. An important aid to increasing your reading comprehension is to read with specific questions in mind. Tell about three other useful suggestions that were offered in this chapter.

Chapter 10

Words: How to Improve Your Knowledge of Them

TRUE CONFESSIONS

1. There is an old joke about a student who looked up the meaning of "to be frugal" and found out that one of the dictionary definitions was "to save." He then used the word in a homework sentence: "When the man fell overboard, he shouted, 'Frugal me!' "

    Have you ever misused a word that way? Tell about it. How could such errors be avoided?

2. What word did you look up in a dictionary lately? Why did you want to know its meaning? How have you used it since you discovered its meaning?

3. A high school senior asked: "Why are teachers always pushing us to use big words? Can't I say the simple word 'cut' or must I use a four-syllable word such as 'laceration'? After all, Ernest Hemingway specialized in words of one syllable, and he was one of America's greatest writers."

    How might a teacher answer that question?

WHY STUDY WORDS?

The purpose of this chapter is to help you increase your vocabulary, adapt it to a more meaningful use, and through that improved use, elevate your grades in school and raise your SAT I scores. As a by-product of a richer vocabulary, you may also take greater delight in the reading that you do for class and for pleasure. Reading not only strengthens your knowledge of word connotations and nuances of meaning, it adds immeasurably to your personal vocabulary.

In this chapter on vocabulary growth you'll find ideas for using a dictionary, suggestions on keeping lists of new words and on putting new words to work. But these are the back-door methods necessary for those who somehow miss the excitement of entering word study by the front door, and the front door of word study is interest. W. H. Auden, the poet, recommended that anyone who wants to be a poet should be able to defend his aspiration by saying: "Because I like to hang around words and overhear them whisper to one another." [1]

THE MANY QUALITIES OF WORDS

Words are the tools of thinking. Beginning with the grunts and exclamations of our remote ancestors, words, these symbols of thought, have flowered into their many uses to provide man with a history totally different from the lower primates. Writes J. Donald Adams:

> In words we reflected all the delights and miseries of human existence. Words are one of the most living things of man's creation; indeed, one might argue that they have more vitality than anything else we have fashioned. What else is there that

---

[1] As quoted by John Ciardi, "Manner of Speaking," *Saturday Review* 55 (March 11, 1972): 14.

seems to lead an independent life? Words do; they acquire strength and lose it; they may, like people, become transformed in character; like certain persons, they may gather evil about them, or like others, prod our wits and lift our hearts.[2]

How particular sounds came to represent particular things is also part of the fascinating story of words. In Plato's shortest dialogue, *Cratylus,* covering only four pages, Socrates speculates on the origin of words. He suggests that many names indicate the nature of the thing named—some names express rest while others show an affinity for motion. The sound of *l* seems to suggest the *lull* that *lures* toward the *lunar* world of rest. How many words with *l* can you list?—leisure, lullaby, lassitude, lazy—the lengthening *list* makes one *listless.* Over against the rest-inducing *l* stands *r,* suggesting motion—run, race, rowdy, rodeo, rattle, ruin, ripple. Ripple, the last mentioned, suggests that some words echo the sound of the thing for which they stand. (The ripples crept quietly under the over-hanging bank. The brook babbled its protest to the rocks as it raced along).

THE ORIGIN OF WORDS

Etymology is the study of the origin and development of a word, says your dictionary, tracing a word as far back as possible. The word etymology comes from two Greek words—*etymon*, meaning "true sense," and *logy*, meaning "the study of." Etymology usually proceeds by the method of linguistic comparisons, indeed, an

[2]J. Donald Adams, *The Magic and Mystery of Words* (New York: Holt, Rinehart and Winston, 1963), 36.

exciting means of discovering the romance behind our everyday language. Add to this the origin of names, and word study takes on an absorbing and fascinating quality found in few subjects.

Think briefly of several names around you. Perhaps there is a mountain named Hawk's Peak, another named Candlewood. Long ago indigenous people may have watched the hawks soar above the peak, brushing the sky with their wings, and named the mountain. And having gone to gather pitch pine to light his frontier cabin, substituting the pine torch for candles, the frontiersman named the mountain where he found the candle wood—Candlewood Mountain.

Etymology, begun with the familiar that lies before your very eyes, and extended to your dictionary, will not only enrich your vocabulary, but will make you word conscious and indirectly improve your ability to read with more comprehension and spell more correctly.

To create a picture of the origin of a single word is to journey into a remote past. The evolution of words reaches far back in time, perhaps eighty thousand years. For many thousands of years signs and grunts named things men saw—slowly language evolved from these mere names of concrete things to expressions of abstract ideas.

About four thousand years ago man advanced his evolution of speech and words into a new epoch; he began to write. First he scratched strangely and crudely on stone, perhaps also with a pointed stick in the sand; afterwards on bits of hardened clay, and finally his materials included papyrus, parchment, and paper. How did he begin? Doubtless with a picture. Slowly the picture came to represent an idea. The idea came to be represented by a symbol—a symbol that could be read and uttered. This was a written word.

Ever since the time of Socrates there have been many theories about the origins of words and names. Was the Native American who looked out from his campsite high on the Blue Ridge Mountains naming the beautiful valley below? Was he echoing the sound of earth and sky caressing at the edge of the vast panorama? Or was he raising his arms in awesome devotion to the daughter-of-the-skies? Anyway, the word he made was—Shen-an-doah, Shenandoah. Is there a single valley on the earth more beautifully named? And what of Je-ru-sa-lem—that beautiful, musical word? How came the word—the name—from David's harp or the wind whispering among the promontory rocks?

THE EXCITEMENT OF WORDS

The excitement of words! A thousand word games, histories, and stories are all about you daily. Do not let the fascination of words be clouded or lost. Every word was in its beginning a stroke of genius. And according to Emerson, "Every word was once a poem." "Uttering a word," said the philosopher Ludwig Wittgenstein, "is like striking a note on the keyboard of the imagination." Words convey most of our ideas and thoughts. Without them we can think only in concrete terms—we can picture an object, a rock, for instance; but we cannot picture an abstraction, such as love. To express the idea of "love" we need words.

The putting together of words to produce distinctive and understandable prose demands sentences that deal quietly and justly with the common feelings of men, and give beauty and loftiness to things of the everyday world—things which, if not lifted up, are sometimes lost in the drab words of grocery lists, small complaints in little language, and repetitions stamped with dullness.

Some of the earth's benefactors came to greatness through their ability to give color, simplicity, enduring strength, and nobility to words. In analyzing the qualities that made Abraham Lincoln great, Benjamin P. Thomas wrote:

> Mastery of language may have been that ultimate factor without which he would have failed. For the self-taught man who once would have given all he owned and gone into debt for the gift of lyric utterance had touched the summits of eloquence. Yet this, like his other achievements, had not come by mere chance. Patient self-training, informed reflection, profound study of a few great works of English literature, esteem for the rhythmic beauty that may be coaxed from language, all these had endowed him with the faculty to write well and to speak well, so that at last, when profound emotions deep within him had felt the impulse of new-born nobility of purpose, they had welled forth—and would well forth once more—in imperishable words.[3]

How then can you put your love of words into action—"to write well and to speak well"? There are four steps: use a dictionary, learn the roots from which many words come, learn prefixes and suffixes, and *use* the words you have learned.

1. USE A DICTIONARY

The first step is to make friends with the dictionary, to make it your lifelong companion. The word "dictionary" is derived from the Latin word *dictio,*

---

[3]Benjamin P. Thomas, *Abraham Lincoln* (New York: Alfred A. Knopf, Inc., 1950), 500.

meaning *to speak*, or *to point out in words*; the dictionary is a book that speaks to us about words. It tells us: a. what are the origins of words, b. how to pronounce them, c. what parts of speech they are, d. how to spell them, e. what their meanings are, f. similar words (synonyms), g. words that have opposite meanings (antonyms). Practice using your dictionary in as thorough a manner as possible. Do not hurry through the entry for the word. Read all the meanings of the word—not merely the first. Try looking at the word *sound* or *round*. The entry for either of these words is very long. You will be surprised to find how many different uses each of these words has.

2. LEARN THE ROOTS OF WORDS

The second part of vocabulary improvement is to learn how to examine the parts of words. Many of the words in the English language have three parts: a prefix, a root, and a suffix. If you learn some prefixes, some roots, and a few suffixes, you can multiply your vocabulary rather than merely add to it word by word.

You would benefit more from memorizing a hundred roots and how to use them than from memorizing five thousand individual words. Of the more than six hundred thousand words in our language, almost half come from about eight hundred roots.

The word *root* is apt, for as the root of a tree supplies the means of growth, so does a knowledge of word roots enable your vocabulary to grow. Not only will you improve your knowledge of meaning but also of spelling. So, take the shortcut to word power—learn roots, and how to use them.

All of the words of English have individual histories, all have origins deep in the past and deep in other languages. The two ancient languages that provide the roots for many of our words are Latin and Greek. Ten Latin verbs provide roots for more than two thousand of our own words.

Latin Verb	Meaning	Roots for English Words
capio	take, seize	cap- (cip-) capt- (cept-)
duco	lead	duct- duc-
facio	do, make	fac- (fic-) fact- (fect-)
fero	carry, bear	fer- lat-
mitto	send	mit- mitt- miss-
plico	fold	-plica- plicat- (plect-) (plex-)
pono	place, put	pon- posit-
tendo	stretch	tend- tent-
teneo	have, hold	tene- tent-
specio	observe, see	spec- (spic-) speci- spect-

Notice that the root *tent-* may come from either of two of the Latin verbs. You will need to remember that as you examine words. For example, from which root does re*tent*ion come, and from which root does con*tent*ion come? The difference in the origin of the roots alters the meaning significantly.

As a beginning to your study of roots, try to find three English words that come from each of the ten Latin verbs.

3. LEARN PREFIXES AND SUFFIXES

The third part of vocabulary building is to learn prefixes and suffixes. These are the parts added to the beginning (prefix) or to the end (suffix) of the root. They will alter the meaning of the word and so

are very important. For example *pre*tend and *in*tend
mean rather different things, even though they come
from the same root. The prefix has made all the
difference.

The following list is of common prefixes and
their meanings. It would be very worth your while
to memorize this list.

Prefix	Meaning	Example
a, ab	from, away	avert, abstain
a, an	without, not	atheist, anarchist
ad, af, at, ag	to	adhere, affix, attain, aggressive
ambi	both	ambidextrous
amphi	around	amphitheater
ant, anti	against	antonym, antipathy
ante	before	antedate
cata	down	cataract, catacomb
con, cor, com	with, together	convene, correlate, compare
contra	against	contradict
de	from, down	descend, debase
di	apart	divert, divorce
dia	through	diameter, diagonal
dis	not	disagree, disappear
e, ex	out of, over	evaluate, exponent
em	out	emanate
em	in	embark
en	in	enclose
hyper	above, over	hypercritical
hypo	under	hypodermic
il	not	illegal, illegible
im	in, not	import, impossible
in	not	inactive

ir	not	irresponsible
per	through	permeate
peri	around	perimeter
post	after	postpone, posterity
pre	before	predict, precede
pro	for, forth	pronoun, procession
re	back, again, down	recall, revive, retreat
sub, sup	under	subordinate, suppose
super	over, above	supervise
trans	across	transport, transmit

Now use the prefixes and the roots to create some words. Check your accuracy with your dictionary. For example, check out: complicate, emit, or reception. How many words can you create?

Suffixes usually tell us how the word is to be used rather than telling us something about its meaning. They tell us whether the word is a noun, an adjective, or a verb, or the comparative degree of an adjective: small*er*, small*est*. Two suffixes may be added to a root to create a word, as in aggress*ively*. You should have a working knowledge of at least the following suffixes.

Suffix	How Word Will Be Used	Meaning	Example
-able, -ible	adjective	capable of	digestible, reliable
-ac, -al, -ial	adjective	pertaining to	cardiac, natural, facial
-acy	noun	pertaining to	legacy
-ance, -ence	noun	state of being	abundance, obedience
-ant, -ent	noun	one who does	servant, student
-er, -or	noun	one who does	actor
-ive	adjective or noun	state of being	aggressive, executive
-ish	adjective	the quality of	mannish
-ity	noun	the quality of	humility
-less	adjective	without	sleepless
-ly	adjective or adverb	like	cheerfully, lovely
-ness	noun	state of	goodness
-ry	noun	state of	rivalry
-ion	noun	act of	tension

This list is by no means exhaustive. At best, it merely suggests what kinds of changes suffixes can make in words.

Now use your knowledge of roots, prefixes, and suffixes to words; for example, missive, permissive, permission, conduct, conductor.

4. USE NEW WORDS

The fourth and final part of vocabulary building is to use the new words you have learned. Incorporate them into your writing for class and into your everyday speech. Without use you will lose the words you have worked to learn.

To make the words familiar friends, strive to memorize them and their meanings. Use new word lists or, far better, new word cards. Keep a list of new words along with their meanings; especially a list of basic vocabulary words that apply to a particular subject, such as biology, chemistry, history, or geometry. The word should be written with the definition that is directed toward the subject. If there are synonyms that help fix the meaning in your mind, they should be written in a column to the right of the definition as here shown:

NEW WORD   DEFINITION   SYNONYM

The card system for new words is, however, greatly recommended. Most students find it more workable and, adaptable. Vocabulary builder cards can be bought. (Try Barron's *SAT I Wordmaster* cards as a start. They contain 600 words you should know, especially if you're preparing for SAT I.) Or, if you want to build your own set, equip yourself with the smallest index cards you can buy—$1\frac{1}{2} \times 3$ or 3×5. Keep them handy as you read or study. When you come upon a new word, write it on the front of the card. On the back write the definition or

definitions, and a synonym or two. Carry half a
dozen or more cards with you, or display them on
your desk, until you have put them in your working
vocabulary; that is, until you are using them in conversation and in your writing. This will seldom take
more than three or four days. The cards may then be
filed alphabetically or by subject vocabulary. Just a
few weeks of practice and the new word cards
become second nature. They can be studied while
riding or walking to and from classes, waiting for a
bus, and at myriad other odd moments, usually lost
and lamented. Put the new word card system to work
to improve your vocabulary and your marks.

PRACTICES FOR VOCABULARY IMPROVEMENT

Use Your Dictionary

When you come upon a new word, a new use for an
old word, a word that you think you know but are not
sure of, reach for your dictionary. Always keep it
within easy reach. Some of your more technical
textbooks may have a glossary at the front or back. The
glossary will provide the meanings of technical words
pertaining to the particular subject, and may also
supply meanings for new scientific words—so new
they are not in your dictionary. The most comprehensive dictionary in the world is the *Oxford English
Dictionary*, affectionately called the OED, a multi-
volume set that can be found in most libraries. For use
at home, you can buy a one-volume OED, which
comes with a high-powered magnifying glass, or wait
for the publication of the OED on CD-ROM, coming
soon. For everyday use, though, nothing beats a good

desktop dictionary, such as the *American College Dictionary* published by Merriam Webster, or the *American Heritage Dictionary of the English Language*. And so that you'll never be out of touch, why not invest in an inexpensive paperback dictionary to stuff in your backpack with your hacky sack and other indispensible gear.

Your dictionary study may lead you to other helpful books: A *Dictionary of Modern English Usage,* H. W. Fowler; Fernald's *Synonyms and Antonyms*; and Roget's *Thesaurus of English Words and Phrases.* The word *thesaurus* comes from the Greek word meaning treasury. Indeed, all dictionaries are treasuries; store-houses not for money but for information.

Avoid Word Blindness

You use some words daily without knowing their full meaning. Some words that you read as part of assign-ments would add much to your understanding of the subject if you really knew them. Try these practices for teaching yourself the exact meanings of familiar words for which you have only vague definitions: a. Begin seeing the word whenever you come upon it. Study how it is used by others. b. Question your own use in comparison with others. c. Use your dictionary to find out if you are getting the most out of the familiar word. d. Apply a specific meaning that will make your algebra, geometry, social studies, easier for you to understand. Vagueness is the curse attending many of the words we use without really knowing.

Become a Word Surgeon

Learn to dissect words into their parts—prefix, root, and suffix. Study word parts until a glance reveals the pattern of the word—whether it is single root, built upon prefix, root, suffix, two roots, or some other combinations. Divide *autobiography, bibliography, pandemonium,* and *transmutation* into word parts. A working knowledge of a few fundamental parts, keen powers of observation, and conscientious practice, is the fast way to add new words to your vocabulary.

Put New Words to Work

Insure a working knowledge by recording each new word along with definition and synonym. A sentence of your own, using the word, is also helpful. New word lists and new word cards are recommended ways of keeping satisfactory records. A word is part of your working vocabulary when you can pronounce it, spell it, and use it in both conversation and writing. New words will not remain alive unless they are allowed to work.

Use the Unlimited Word-world of Fascination that Surrounds You on all Sides

John Ruskin defined genius as "a superior power of seeing." Why not use this definition to give yourself the quality of genius in word study? Exercise that "superior power of seeing" to enjoy for the first time place names, your own names, words derived from people's names, trade names, words that name our foods, our days, our weeks, our months, our seasons, and how about your own last name? Make a game of improving your vocabulary and the ability to use that vocabulary. "To carry the feelings of childhood into the powers of manhood," said Coleridge, "to combine the child's sense of wonder and novelty with the appearance which every day for years has rendered familiar, that is the character and privilege of genius. . . ." Keep "the child's sense of wonder and novelty" for your word study.

LOOKING BACK

1. One of the best ways to broaden your vocabulary is to consult a dictionary frequently in order to find the meaning of unfamiliar words. What are the three other suggestions for expanding your word knowledge that were mentioned in this chapter?

2. On the verbal part of SAT I, you will find two sections that, among other things, will put your vocabulary to the test:[4]

A. Sentence completion.

Lavish in visual beauty, the film *Lawrence of Arabia* also boasts ———— of style: it knows how much can be shown in a shot, how much can be said in a few words.

(A) extravagance (B) economy (C) autonomy
(D) frivolity (E) arrogance

B. Verbal analogies.

TACITURNITY: LACONIC::
   (A) improvisation:unrehearsed
   (B) verbosity: pithy
   (C) silence: golden
   (D) ballet:ungainly
   (E) vacation:leisurely

---

[4]Examples from Samuel C. Brownstein and Sharon Green, *How to Prepare for SAT I* (Hauppauge, NY: Barron's) 1997.

How would you go about picking the right answers to these questions if you didn't know the exact meaning of every word?

What answers would you give if you were tested on the words *biped, retrogress, matriarchy*?

3. "Some of the earth's benefactors came to greatness through their ability to give color, simplicity, enduring strength, and nobility to words."

The above quotation comes from Chapter 11 and will, no doubt, remind you of Churchill, Lincoln, and other great wordsmiths who have been mentioned in this book. Can you name three contemporaries who use language skillfully? Think of newspaper columnists, TV personalities, lyricists for rock groups, your friends and teachers. Can you quote some of their most memorable lines?

Chapter 11

Written Work: The Product and Its Package

TRUE CONFESSIONS

1. When your teacher returns a graded paper or essay to you and it's filled with corrections and bears a low grade, what do you do? Examine it carefully, tear it up, hide it and read it later when no one is around? Do you try to take advantage of the comments on your papers, or do you view them as a sadistic form of harrassment?

2. At the start of English class, Mr. Snyder distributed paper for a brief writing assignment on a short story in Raymond Carver's *Cathedral*. Several students asked, "Does this count?"

   Would you have been likely to ask that question? How do experienced teachers usually respond to the question?

3. "I know that the paper I handed in was sloppy looking, but I think that teachers ought to be more concerned with content than with looks. Anyway, my printer is all messed up, so that's why my paper looks bad. If I get a failing grade because of that, I'm going to complain."

   Tell why you would or would not support such a protest.

THE NATURE OF THE PRODUCT

Of the several skills you will develop in educating yourself—listening, reading, speaking, thinking, and writing—the one that will give your teachers the widest range for measuring your ability and achievements will be your writing. While preparing a piece of written work for a course, you may talk over your idea with others, you may write a draft or two that your classmates may scrutinize, you may even ask for help in resolving a sticky problem of usage or meaning. Nevertheless, the product you ultimately hand in to your teacher for a grade is yours alone and reflects on your qualities as a student. When reading your piece, the teacher will not be judging your friends, your classmates, the librarian who gave you help, but you and you alone.

Your skill in writing will, fortunately or unfortunately, affect what your teachers in every school subject think of your work; because it is largely in writing that you demonstrate what you have learned. Writing, to some extent, also reveals more of your character, your willingness to pursue excellence or accept mediocrity, than perhaps any other of your school work. It is, in fact, the most important product that you have to sell. You sell it, not for dollars and cents, but for a grade. As with any other product, the quality product brings the quality price.

The pricing does not begin with the term paper or the big test or essay. Your saleable written product begins with the daily paper, be it two sentences, a list of ten words, or five problems in mathematics. It includes not only English papers, as many students mistakenly think, but lab reports, all test papers, homework assignments, research papers, responses to reading, and in some schools, a senior paper of perhaps five to ten thousand words.

The primary purpose of all written work is to impart information and to develop thought. Ideally, whatever you submit for evaluation should be (1) clear, (2) interesting, (3) enlightening, (4) correct, and (5) attractive. To be sure, not all your assignments can be judged by all five criteria. A group of math problems or a list of vocabulary words will be measured only by their degree of correctness and attractiveness; attractiveness being accomplished by neatness and arrangement. A list of ten words strung across the page, unnumbered, illegibly written, means something quite different to the teacher than does a list numbered down the page in a straight column, neat and legible—reflecting care. Five problems arranged on a paper for symmetry and neatness, each problem distinctly numbered, each answer marked for easy identification, bring a better price than the indifferent, sloppy paper, even though both papers might have the correct answers.

Certain obligations are basic to all writers, regardless of their talent: (1) For each written assignment writers should make the necessary study and inquiry to have a working knowledge of the subject about which they are writing. (2) They should present information in a fluent and effective vocabulary, coherent and unified sentence and paragraph structure, and the greatest degree of mechanical perfection possible. (3) And most important of all is the obligation never to try to pass off thoughtless, trite, boring, and sloppy written work with no aim beyond that of getting by.

All effective written composition presupposes having something to say, although there is among some students the feeling that to be seen on record is sufficient. Being seen on record merely means filling up space with writing. Space fillers not infrequently are the same people whose handwriting, almost impossible to read, is deliberately designed to obscure thought and meaning rather than reveal it. Or they have become adept at submitting handsomely decorated covers for their essays and reports that seem to have served only to divert their energies from the writing task at hand. Inside, their papers are crammed with pages of such unsubstantiated generalities and other forms of worthless, cut-rate, and meaningless rubbish that teachers cringe at the thought of having to grade them. In contrast, students who understand the importance of clear thinking and writing will submit papers that have been so carefully and refreshingly prepared that teachers will actually look forward to the experience of reading them.

If your written work is not clearly understandable, and in the form of which you are capable, your teacher will detect it in the first paper you write. If you write on a subject about which you have no sound knowledge, you are a dishonest pretender. If you know your subject but do not bother to express your thoughts in the best possible form, your behavior is irresponsible. Thus, your whole attitude and character are revealed.

WRITING THEMES, OR COMPOSITIONS

Themes are written compositions that require more than a paragraph or two. Themes fall generally into two classes, either a composition of ideas or a composition of images.

The composition of ideas deals with relating information and expounding thought. It would include what is usually classified as expository and argumentative writing, such as essays, and long examination answers. Themes growing out of history and science assignments would fall in this class.

The theme of images is generally what would be expected as an assignment associated with an English course, although in advanced English courses themes of criticism and explanation would fall in the classification of ideas. The composition of images deals with narrative and descriptive writing, and may take the form of story, description, poetry, or drama.

FIVE STEPS IN THEME WRITING

This is not to imply that all students are supposed to become instant, talented writers, possessing unusual creative ability. Whatever your talents, you can improve your writing of themes by following four steps: (1) Choosing the subject or, if assigned by the teacher, deciding upon the point of view. (2) Making an outline; studying, and revising the outline. (3) Writing the first copy, making outline revisions if necessary. (4) Writing the final copy.

The subject you select can influence in many ways the mark you get. Students often make the mistake of choosing one of these five dangerous types of topics:

1. One that is too broad—*The Roaring Twenties* rather than *After the Gulf War*.
2. A topic that is too trite—*My Summer Vacation* rather than *Windsurfing on Long Island Sound*.

3. A topic that is too personal and in questionable taste—*My Two-Timing Father* rather than *Computer Nerds.*
4. A topic that may be too controversial for the reader to maintain objectivity—*Why Teacher Tenure Doesn't Work* rather than *The Zen of Lawn Mowing.*
5. A topic that requires too much background research—*Airline Safety* rather than *Shopping at the Gap.*

The troubles arising from choosing a topic that is too broad are immediately evident. Nothing worthwhile can be said in six hundred or a thousand words on a topic that would require a volume for intelligent coverage. The big topic for a short theme usually ends in generalizations reflecting the writer's lack of information and forcing the teacher to reread stale and tired facts known by everyone.

Childish topics are sometimes chosen to avoid any hard thinking. *What I Did Last Summer* or *What I Think About Getting My Senior License,* may be cute, but unless such topics are handled in a fresh and unique way, they are apt to be clichés. To write your thoughts about a highly personal topic may be good therapy, but it may show poor judgment. While every topic has its time and place, is an essay for English class an appropriate place for airing your thoughts on a drug problem or your parents' divorce? An apt personal experience, however, can be used effectively for illustration or for an example to prove a point. But it should be well thought out and simply presented.

Controversial topics can quickly lose all objectivity and become subject to personal feelings. Other people do not necessarily share your feelings and prejudices.

Teachers grading your paper would not consciously give a lower grade for ideas with which they were not in agreement, but it is wise to remember that judgment is not immune to the weaknesses of human nature.

If you are like most students, your time is precious. Choosing a topic that requires a great deal of background research can be worthwhile but very time consuming. Rather than write a theme which rings hollow and superficial because you haven't had time to learn about it in depth, choose a topic with which you are familiar. Dip into your well of experience and present data that you already know. Without consulting a book or computer, you are an expert on many topics pertaining to the life of the teenagers in your school, for example.

If the topic is assigned, you have no problems; if not, there are intelligent approaches to selecting a topic. One excellent approach is to consult general sources of information, such as an encyclopedia, to find out about a subject that interests you. Suppose you are interested in black holes in space. By checking the encyclopedia, you might find information about them and also references to other sources of information. You would need to narrow your topic, perhaps by choosing to concentrate on one of the noted astronomers or the methods used in the search for black holes. If either of these topics appeared too broad, further reading would help you to narrow the topic. The encyclopedia, however, is always a good place to start.

In selecting a topic for image composition, choose from the world immediately before you. You will write a better paper and get a higher grade for a description of a gnarled and ancient sycamore tree outside your window than for a storm at sea that you have not experienced.

The second progression toward a perfect theme is an outline. Perhaps you have had the experience of writing a paragraph and then remembering something you wish you had included; not too important, but significant enough to have added to the unity and contributed to the completeness of the thought. When you write in longhand, an outline can save you much regret, rewriting, and copying. Because paragraphs usually require a definite pattern and structure, the questions for it become doubly important. On the other hand, if you are accustomed to using a word processor, sorting and rearranging ideas is no problem at all. In fact, organizing your piece of writing may happen simultaneously with composing it. Nevertheless, thinking about paragraph construction and arrangement is essential for all writers, regardless of the medium they use.

Here are some questions to ask yourself as you write:

1. Do I have a complete mental blueprint of what this paragraph is to contain?
2. What topic sentence do I want to convey the topic clearly to my reader?
3. What paragraph pattern will best develop the topic?
4. Will my arrangement of ideas lead naturally from main to supporting ideas?
5. Will my choice of words make my meaning clear?
6. Will this paragraph contain only the material necessary to picture the thought or answer completely?
7. Will it be judged as distinctive quality writing or muddled generalization that is devoid of value?
8. Will my concluding statement (summary sentence) convince my reader of my ability to control, condense, and keep meaningful structure to the end?

It might surprise and even annoy you that a simple paragraph demands such planning. Perhaps incentive to undertake these practices may come from the realization that you will probably be marked on hundreds of single paragraph test answers before you finish your schooling. It might also be remembered that whether you write a two or ten thousand-word theme, the total merit will be measured by the quality of the sentence first, and the paragraph next.

If it is necessary to outline (blueprint orally) even a paragraph, good common sense says that a composition of any length will not fall into order without a plan. Main topics should be recorded first. After the main topics have been shuffled into the order that will produce the best emphasis, coherence, and unity, the supporting topics may then be outlined. The nature of the theme will dictate the order of the outline— chronological, numerical, alphabetical, place, or some other logical order that you have devised to fit the topic.

Do not be afraid to spend some time on the outline. It will be saved later on the writing, and the product will be more orderly and complete. Many professional writers spend as much time outlining as they spend in actual writing. You can train yourself to outline orally as you go to and from school, or while you are jogging or riding your bike. This will save you much time. One writer of academic books outlines each chapter while chopping wood.

Even though you might change the outline some- what after you start to write, outlining one or two themes will convince you of its many advantages. It prevents mistakes in the selection and arrangement of material and insures a sensible proportion of main and contributing ideas. One of the greatest advantages to outlining is that it leads to the discovery of new ideas, new ways to illustrate a point, and a new sense of unity.

A careful examination of the completed outline is always helpful. Here again, questions are a good method of testing whether or not the outline does what you expect of it: (1) Will the outline move the theme directly forward and hold the interest of the reader? (2) Is the outline sufficiently planned and clear for the reader to see it beneath the content? (3) Is the outline free of contradictions and repetitions? (4) Does the outline unite main topics in such a way as to make the message of the whole theme possible in a sentence or two, and certainly not more than a brief paragraph?

The outline thus examined, you are ready for the next major step in theme writing: composing the first draft. If you write in longhand, be sure to leave room for making changes and corrections by leaving every other line blank.

Some writers do their best work by writing their first draft as rapidly as they can. Others try to make their first drafts as nearly like the final product as possible. Each method has its pluses and minuses.

Rapid writing gives a spontaneity that will add life to your composition. Rapidity will also give your writing a flowing movement forward, whereas slow writing will move only by jerks. Rapid writing may also dictate changes in your outline that will improve your theme. Do not be afraid to make such changes, for blind affection to the outline can cause stiff and lifeless spots in your composition. By writing rapidly, ideas may fall more readily into their proper place, but the mechanics of writing are often given short shrift. Since the first draft may be crowded with errors, students may need to spend considerable time making corrections in subsequent drafts.

Slower writers often avoid many mechanical errors. Because they may reread what they have written as they go from paragraph to paragraph, they also may endow their work with a greater unity than does the more slapdash writer. On the other hand, the slow writer who has struggled over words, crossed out words, confused sentence constructions, and fragmentized ideas by changes finds revision a major job, equivalent to rewriting the whole theme.

The fourth and final step in good composition writing is the production of the final copy. If possible, have a time lapse between the working draft and the final copy. This period for generally thinking over and around the topic will usually result in ideas to clear up difficult spots, in decisions over choice of words, and in the detection of mechanical mistakes made in earlier drafts.

In the final draft be concerned for the format and general appearance of the paper. Ask yourself the twelve questions of good essay writing that appear on pages 116 and 117 of this book. Also, anticipate what your teacher is likely to think about your paper. Does your paper suggest that you are one of those exceptional students who take great pride in their work and are willing to devote extra time and energy to demonstrate that they sincerely care about high-quality performance?

THE NATURE OF THE PACKAGE

Nothing in a teacher's experience is more rewarding than to receive a written paper of such neatness and quality as to wish that it did not end. On the other side of the card, it is equally true that nothing can cause the teacher so much frustration, such feeling of ineffective teaching, and such painful, exasperating waste of time as a paper that shows concern for neither form nor content.

The trite and the ordinary, the mediocre and the humdrum, the boring and the unorganized, reveal a total indifference to clarity, form, style, and quality. Neglect of grammar, spelling, punctuation, vocabulary, and legibility stamps the writer as one whose chief aim is to get by and whose highest standard of measurement is accepted incompetence. From this the teacher can easily judge that completely lacking in the writer is any element of appreciation for excellence or even an honest desire to be one's better self.

Does your work reveal a sense of pride in presentation that cannot be hidden, regardless of whether or not all your answers are correct and your thinking clear? If the assignment is a six hundred-word essay, do you crudely jot down the number of words at the end of each page, finally reaching, for you, the great climax of 608, an insult to your reader. Is your paper as neat as you can possibly make it, or is it in pencil when asked for in ink or typed, and in your illegible scribble that you mistakenly believe can be read by others because you can decipher it? What of the student who, writing on the laws of Hammurabi, misspells Hammurabi in the title of his paper and then alternates between correct and incorrect for the remainder of the paper? What of the person who brings his paper a day late or even an hour late? What of the American history student who, assigned a three thousand-word theme, turns in a disorganized fifteen hundred words, and asked "Why?" by his teacher, replies, "I guess I wasn't interested enough," How very sad! What was lacking? A sense of pride, without which there is no excellence. For excellence is reaching beyond the little self, going beyond the narrow circumference that stifles and retards the lesser and the average.

It is all very simple. If you accept the "minimum" as a standard, you will get a minimum mark. If you require excellence of yourself, you will get an excellent mark. The same reflections will be mirrored in life after you have completed your studies. Unless your sense of pride demands excellence of you, you might be lucky and make an exciting sale or bring in a big account, but the way you write the report will reveal your character. If you are not promoted, the answer is within you. You need not ask your employer, "Why?"

IMPROVING YOUR WRITING

Many students misunderstand the basic purpose of theme assignments, and as a result miss the most important contribution that such assignments make to their education. The primary purpose is not a grade, although one should always strive to get the best grade possible. The first objective is to help the student gain proficiency in writing; this can only be achieved if the criticisms given by the teacher are carefully noted and if a sincere effort is made not to repeat the same shortcomings again and again.

If you can remember your last theme grade, but do not know the specific weaknesses or strengths that brought about the grade, you are among those who miss the purpose of theme assignments. When a theme is returned to you, keep it in writing folder or portfolio. When your next theme is assigned, check your weaknesses from the last one before you start to write. A list of types of mistakes and shortcomings and the frequency with which they occurred on successive themes offers graphic incentive for improvement.

By studying the mistakes you make frequently on two or three themes, you can make yourself an improvement chart or "rubric" to fit your needs. It might appear as follows, although its categories would be tailored to your needs:

SAMPLE RUBRIC FOR EVALUATING A THEME

Types of Errors & Weaknesses Noted	Number of Times Occurring					
	1st Week	2nd Week	3rd Week	4th Week	5th Week	6th Week

Whole essay
  Clarity of main idea
  Focus/Unity/Purpose
  Overall organization
  Economy of expres-
    sion						

Paragraphs
  Topic sentences
  Development of
    ideas
  Use of transitions
  Arrangement of
    ideas						

Sentences
  Variety
  Sentence errors
    Run-ons
    Fragments
    Comma splices						

Word choice
  Appropriateness
  Interest						

Usage and Grammar						

Mechanics
  Spelling
  Punctuation						

Mark received						

Overall Criticism Teacher's Comments	First Week
	Second Week
	Third Week
	Fourth Week
	Fifth Week
	Sixth Week

Certainly, there are few among us who do not enjoy evidence of self-improvement. The improvement chart, listing your particular shortcomings, can be used to encourage and record your improvement. If your particular faults can be pinpointed, it will be wise to include them specifically rather than under a general entry. For example, if you make apostrophe and semicolon mistakes more often than others, make individual entries for these under punctuation. Your teachers could probably give valuable help in preparing your chart.

Teachers also can give valuable help if you go to your teacher after class with a paper in hand and ask for extra help. Ask the teacher to show you how to express more clearly or economically what you have tried to say in your paper. In this way you will see how better to arrange your topic or better to express yourself about your topic. If you do not go with paper in hand, your teacher will be glad to help you, but may supply personal examples. It is more helpful to have the examples come from your own paper; you will understand them better and be better able to apply the lessons you learn to your other writing. Going to ask for help from your teacher with your work in hand also will show that you honestly wish to improve and are not asking in order to make a good impression.

HOW TO JUDGE QUALITY

Whether written work takes the form of a single sentence to answer a question, a simple paragraph, or a long theme, the primary requirements are demanded of the writer. Perhaps one of the best methods of producing quality writing is to always approach it with questions, and judge it by questions when it is written.

Ask yourself the following questions about the next one- or two-sentence answers you write. Use these only as beginners, and add questions of your own. Make them progressively demanding until you feel that you have acquired the ability to sense and produce quality answers, and to detect and avoid worthless quantity. Can I start my answer by restating the idea of the question, and thereby make it easy for the reader to mark my paper? Will I carefully avoid using a pronoun to replace the subject of the question? Does this answer contain the fewest number of words possible to make a quality answer? Is this a generalization that does not answer the question, but is a dishonest attempt to get by? These four questions can change the nature both of the answers you write for tests, and of the themes you write. Copy each on a 3 × 5 index card, and ask your teacher if you can keep them before you as you take quizzes and tests.

SUGGESTIONS FOR IMPROVING WRITTEN WORK

➤ Written work reveals ability and motivation. It is the most important product you have to offer in exchange for a grade.

➤ The primary aims of all written work are: (1) to impart information and (2) to develop thought. Work submitted for evaluation should be (1) clear, (2) interesting, (3) enlightening, (4) correct, and (5) attractive.

➤ Judge the quality of written composition by questioning its parts, content, and presentation.

➤ Observe closely the three basic responsibilities of all students toward written work:
   a. Must have a working knowledge of the subject.
   b. Must present the material in the best possible form and structure.
   c. Must avoid the habit of passing off inferior work in the hopes of getting by.

➤ Excellence in performance comes from a sense of pride in one's work.

➤ Adopt practices that will reveal weaknesses and inspire improvement. Beginning with the four steps in good composition writing, plot your own methods for adding quality and completeness.

LOOKING BACK

1. In deciding on a theme for your health class, four titles come to mind:
   a. Maintaining Good Health
   b. Why Smoking Is Bad for You

c. My Fight Against Depression

d. Teenagers' Sleeping Disorders

Which one would you select? Why? Which is the poorest choice you could have made? Why?

2. In this chapter, four steps in theme writing are discussed:

a. Pick the best topic

b. Prepare an outline

c. Write a first draft

d. Write a final copy

Which is the most important step?

3. The opening sentence of this chapter is: "Of the several skills you will develop in educating yourself—listening, reading, speaking, thinking, and writing—the one that will give your teachers the widest range for measuring your ability and achievements will be your writing."

Tell whether you agree with the statement. Why?

Select one of the other skills and explain why that one is the most significant for the career you are planning.

Chapter 12
....
Written Work: Style and Usage

TRUE CONFESSIONS

1. Do you remember Winston Churchill's famous reference to "wounds, unrelenting labor, perspiration, and weeping"? Of course you don't, because Churchill used "blood, toil, sweat, and tears" in his stirring speech to his countrymen.

    Why all the fuss over Churchill's choice of words? Did they really matter? Why? What makes one slogan more memorable than another?

2. Some years ago an advertising copywriter was preparing an ad for Ivory soap. In two hundred words he told about the "unique saponification" of Ivory, and how it was engineered to stay atop the water "during one's ablutions." His boss studied the results, then drew a red line through the whole article and replaced it with two words: "It floats!"

    Was the boss' revision an improvement? Tell why?

3. Have you ever uttered sentences similar to those below?
    a. They say it will rain today.
    b. He's very fickle, they say, and won't go out with the same girl for more than a few weeks.
    c. They say she's a terrible mother who actually neglects her children.

Do you see anything wrong with such statements? If so, why do people use them?

MODELS OF GOOD STYLE

Written work is critical to your success in school. You cannot escape it—you must write not only in English class, but also in history, science, math, and foreign language classes. Now that we have examined theme writing in some detail, let us turn to the examination of style and usage.

Do pomposity, ostentation, pretentiousness, and ornamentation—fringed with the gingerbread of garbled and garish vocabulary—produce the word pictures that give meaning and understanding to our thoughts? Are not, rather, clarity, simplicity, sincerity, and order—whose by-product is beauty—the things for which we aim? Is this not the pattern of all deathless utterances that are our heritage and our models?

Let's examine what some of the world's great thinkers have written to see how their prose works. Thucydides, the Greek historian, writing a history of the Peloponnesian War, wrote in "such a way," said Plutarch, "as to make his hearer a spectator." Here is the beginning paragraph of Thucydides' description of the deadly plague that ravaged Athens in 429 B.C., carrying away half the population of the city, among whom was the city's foremost leader—Pericles. Note the simplicity of the words used. Not a single technical or medical term appears in the whole three-page description of the disease, yet doctors are able to diagnose the epidemic from symptoms so clearly described. Here follows a single paragraph:

Words indeed fail one when one tries to give a general picture of this disease; and as for the sufferings of individuals, they seemed almost beyond the capacity of human nature to endure. Here in particular is a point where this plague showed itself to be something quite different from ordinary diseases: though there were many dead bodies lying about unburied, the birds and animals that eat human flesh either did not come near them or, if they did taste the flesh, died of it afterwards. Evidence for this may be found in the fact that there was a complete disappearance of all birds of prey: they were not to be seen either round the bodies or anywhere else. But dogs, being domestic animals, provided the best opportunity of observing this effect of the plague.[1]

Sophocles, listed always among the world's greatest dramatists, has the following description of man at the end of the first scene in his play, *Antigone:*

There are many wonderful things, but none more wonderful than man. Over the whitecaps of the sea he goes, driven by the stormy winds, topped by the towering waves; and the Earth, oldest of the gods, eternal and tireless, he wears away, turning furrows with his plow year after year. He snares the light-hearted birds and the wild beasts of the fields, and he catches in his nets the fish of the sea, man forever resourceful. He tames the animals that roam the meadows and mountains, yoking the shaggy horses and the powerful bulls. And he has learned the use of language to express wind-swift thought,

[1]Thucydides, Book 2, 50. As translated by Rex Warner, *Thucydides, The Peloponnesian War* (Baltimore: Penguin, 1954), 125.

and he has mastered the art of living with other men in addition to the conquest of nature. Skillfully he meets the future; although he has found no escape from death, he has discovered release from painful diseases. His ingenuity results in evil as well as good; when he respects his country's laws and justice he deserves honor; but may the arrogant man, untrue to his city, never come to my hearth or share my thoughts.[2]

In the corridor of the library of Cambridge University hangs a small frame, enclosing a short speech of two hundred eighty-seven words. Under the frame is a placard with the inscription: THE NOBLEST PROSE EVER WRITTEN. The speech is:

Fourscore and seven years ago our fathers brought forth on this continent a new nation, conceived in liberty, and dedicated to the proposition that all men are created equal.

Now we are engaged in a great civil war, testing whether that nation, or any nation so conceived and so dedicated, can long endure. We are met on a great battle-field of that war. We have come to dedicate a portion of that field as a final resting-place for those who here gave their lives that that nation might live. It is altogether fitting and proper that we should do this.

But, in a larger sense, we cannot dedicate—we cannot consecrate—we cannot hallow—this ground. The brave men, living and dead, who struggled here, have consecrated it far above our poor power to add or detract. The world will little note nor

---

[2]Sophocles, *Antigone*, II. 333–373. As translated by Walter R. Agard, *The Greek Mind* (Princeton: D. Van Nostrand Co. Inc., 1957), 143.

long remember what we say here, but it can never forget what they did here. It is for us, the living, rather, to be dedicated here to the unfinished work which they who fought here have thus far so nobly advanced. It is rather for us to be here dedicated to the great task remaining before us—that from these honored dead we take increased devotion to that cause for which they gave the last full measure of devotion; that we here highly resolve that these dead shall not have died in vain; that this nation, under God, shall have new birth of freedom; and that government of the people, by the people, for the people, shall not perish from the earth.[3]

On November 19, 1863, a national cemetery was being dedicated at Gettysburg, Pennsylvania, where during the first three days of the previous July, thousands of soldiers had died. Senator Edward Everett was the principal speaker at the dedication. He dealt with concepts of government, the evolution of democracy, and many other profound abstractions for an hour and fifty-five minutes. The world has forgotten what he said, but it remembers 265 words of Lincoln's Gettysburg Address. Why? Because seldom in history have words been guided by the mind to produce such clarity, simplicity, sincerity, and ordered beauty.

As we turn to look at the uses to which words can be put, the attributes they take on, and how you can make them work best for you, keep constantly in mind the four qualities found in the models just observed: (1) clarity, (2) simplicity, (3) sincerity, and (4) order— which by arrangement produce beauty. These should

---

[3]Abraham Lincoln, *The Collected Writings of Abraham Lincoln*, ed. Ray P. Baslen, 9 vols. (New Brunswick: Rutgers Univ. Press, 1953), 7:23.

stand guard over whatever you speak or write, and should be the primary elements of your style. These are the qualities that your teachers, your readers, and your listeners expect to find as you express your thoughts.

CLARITY

To put it simply, clarity is saying exactly what you mean to say. Be aware of the denoted and the connoted meanings of words. Denoted meanings are the primary, explicit definitions that a dictionary gives. Connoted meanings are the ones that have, through custom and use, come to be associated to a word. When you use a word, all the denotations and connotations will cluster around it, ready to confuse an unwary reader.

As a reader of this book, you are probably one of those persons described as a teenager, an adolescent, a young adult, a youth, a minor, a juvenile, a post-pubescent, a preadult. Do you see any differences among these labels? How would you clarify the differences among them to a foreigner just learning to speak English? Do you like or dislike any of them? Are there any other words that are missing from this list?

Here is a classic anecdote on the need for clarity:[4]

> A foreign-born plumber in New York City wrote to the Federal Bureau of Standards that he had found hydrocloric acid did a good job of cleaning out clogged drains.
>
> The bureau wrote, "The efficacy of hydrochloric acid is indisputable, but the corrosive residue is incompatible with metallic permanence."

---

[4]Richard D. Altick, *Preface to Critical Reading,* 4th ed. (Austin, TX: Holt, Reinhart, Winston, 1962), 87.

The plumber replied he was glad the bureau agreed.

Again the bureau wrote, "We cannot assume responsibility for the production of toxic and noxious residue with hydrochloric acid and suggest you use an alternative procedure."

The plumber was happy again at bureau agreement with his idea.

Then the bureau wrote, "Don't use hydrochloric acid. It eats the hell out of pipes."

Do you choose your words carefully—you may not lose a court case, but you may lose points on an essay because of poor word choice.

Try a little practice at examining connotations. Examine the word *mark*.

MEANING	USE
Denoted: to make a mark (verb)	Mark your notebook for easy identification.
a line, dot, etc. (noun)	Who put the mark on the desk?
Connoted: to wait	He will mark time until summer.
a sign or indication	The ability to listen is the mark of a civilized man.
to listen, heed	Mark my words, he will not return.
a sign of evil	He is cursed with the mark of Cain.
a standard of quality	This paper is not up to the mark.
importance, distinction	The chairman is a man of mark.

impression	He left his mark on his students.
a guide or point of reference	The harbor lights were a mark for fliers.
a target	He did not hit the mark.
an aim, goal	The mark of the campaign was to raise six thousand dollars.
a nautical term	Bits of leather indicated the marks on the sounding line. Samuel Clemens adopted the riverboat call "mark twain" as his pen name.
to show plainly	Her smile marked her happiness.
to be ready	I am on my mark.

See how many connoted meanings you can find for the following familiar words:

> term, take, tag, table, tack, sweep, snap, spread, train, and pick

Now try the simple word *run,* it has more than a dozen connoted meanings. Write your own meaning for each use as shown in the sentences that follow:

1. The boys have the *run* of the club.
   Meaning:

2. The bus *runs* past the store,
   Meaning:

3. The depression caused a *run* on the banks.
   Meaning:

4. She got a *run* in her stocking from kneeling.
   Meaning:

5. He *runs* the assembly with an iron hand.
   Meaning:

6. The dog *run* in our backyard provided exercise for our terrier.
   Meaning:

7. *Cats* has had one of the longest *runs* in theatrical history.
   Meaning:

8. Mo Vaughn hit another home *run* last night.
   Meaning:

9. The mayor had a close *run* in the election.
   Meaning:

10. The fishermen had a *run* of good luck on trout.
    Meaning:

11. The broker *runs* up a big telephone bill.
    Meaning:

12. Anton *ran* the spear through the door.
    Meaning:

13. Cleveland *ran* for president twice.
    Meaning:

14. Pasteur *ran* down the cause of the silkworms dying in Provençal.
    Meaning:

Distinctive use lifts the common and familiar out of the realm of the ordinary. Great improvement in ability to handle words can be derived by practice in replacing many overused and tired words with more pointed and graphic connotative substitutes. Read with a keen eye for finding new uses for the many words which heretofore have had only one or two meanings for you.

Meanings can be made clear by examining the use of the word in the sentence. A word may have meanings that are almost opposite, as shown by the uses of *fast* in this sentence: The torpedo was *fast* approaching its target; seconds before it had been *fast* in its tube. The first connotes great speed, and the second implies being held motionless. As with new words, new meanings must be put to work if you expect to keep them in your vocabulary.

In addition to choosing words carefully for the purpose of clarity, you must also choose clear sentence structure. Long, complex sentences can be difficult to understand because of the thicket of clauses the reader must hack his way through. Make the subjects stand out in sentences, make the modifiers clearly modify what you want them to. Avoid, however, simplistic sentences that pile upon one another lifelessly. Find a middle ground, neither too flowery nor too simple— but above all be clear.

SIMPLICITY

Simplicity is the using of ordinary words and ordinary structures of grammar. It is not the writing of slang and common abbreviations to shorten your work. Too often, poor writers lapse into slang and clichés when writing, without recognizing what they are doing. Some students, on the other hand, appear fond of words of many syllables and use them even when short, memorable ones are suitable. In your writing prefer simple, concrete words to vague, complex ones: *run* or *walk* instead of *move, group* instead of *assemblage, then* instead of *at that point in time.*

The world knows no force sufficient to stand against the power of simple words. As the strength of a parachute is derived from each tiny thread, so is the strength of ideas dependent upon each fragile verbal tool that is used to express the idea. The strength and completeness of each comment you make in class, each question you ask, each answer you write on tests will depend upon how wisely you choose your words.

Perhaps you've heard of Wee Willie Keeler, a hard-hitting outfielder for the New York Giants about a hundred years ago. When asked the secret of his success as a batter, thank goodness Willie didn't say, "I swing my bat and launch the spheroidal projectile to areas of the playing field devoid of defensive players." No, Willie knew the power of keeping it simple and said, "I hit 'em where they ain't."

Once you have chosen simple, direct words, use a simple grammatical structure to combine those words in sentences. Avoid piling clause upon clause—if you find yourself writing a sentence which is too long or complex, break it up into two or more shorter and simpler sentences. At the same time, do not use such a multitude of short declarative sentences that you bore your reader.

In addition to care in word choice and sentence structure, choose carefully the voice of your verbs. The most important characteristic of life is action, and speaking and writing that reflect the thoughts of life most effectively do so through action. For that reason, it is always better to use the active rather than passive voice of verbs. To say "Fishing is enjoyed by John" (passive voice), leaves John motionless; but to say "John enjoys fishing" (active voice), starts him on his way, making the subject act upon something.

After the subject, which is the reason for the thought being expressed, the *verb* is *the important word.* It carries the weight, contains the vigor, and, if carefully chosen, is capable of sound and color. Note the verbs in the sentences that follow:

1. The USSR *declined* rapidly after the failed coup of 1991; both political and economic strength were gone.
2. The USSR was *doomed* after the failed coup of 1991; disorder, debility, and despair prevailed.

Even though the verb *declined* is given a modifier to speed the action, it does not bring the USSR crashing with the resounding sense and sound of *doom*. And what of *were gone* as compared with *prevailed*? The tense of *were gone* removes the action of political and economic strength, but there remained action—disorder, debility, and despair *prevailed*.

CHOOSING ACTIVE WORDS

One of the glorious achievements of man, said Sophocles, was that "he has learned the use of language to express windswift thought."[5] Another translation puts it in slightly different word:

> Words also, and thought as rapid as air,
> He fashions to his good use.[6]

Which words impress us most when we hear or read them? Surely, those that produce action and bring a thought to life. Words, which, as Sophocles puts it, are active enough to express thoughts as swift as wind.

Of all the parts of speech, verbs carry more action than the others. Active verbs stimulate reader interest.

---

[5]Sophocles, *Antigone*, trans. Agard, 143.
[6]Sophocles, *Antigone*, 1. 353. As translated by Dudley Fitts, *Greek Plays in Modern Translation* (New York: Dial Press, 1947), 470.

They perform, stir up, get up and move around. They excel in their power to pump vitality into your writing. They add energy and variety to sentences. As a bonus, active verbs often help you trim needless words from your writing.

In contrast, being verbs are stagnant. They don't do anything. Notice the lifelessness in all the most common forms of the verb *to be: is, are, was, were, am, has been, had been, will be.* When used in a sentence, each of these being verbs joins the subject to the predicate—and that's all. In fact, the verb *to be* acts much like an equal sign in an equation, as in "Four minus three *is* one" ($4 - 3 = 1$), "Harold *is* smart" (Harold = smart), or "Coke *is* the real thing" (Coke = RT). Because equal signs (and being verbs) show no action, use active verbs whenever you can.

Of course, being verbs are perfectly acceptable in speech and writing. You can't get along without them, but use them sparingly. If more than 25 percent of your sentences use a being verb, you may be relying on them too heavily.

Substitute active verbs for being verbs by extracting them from other words in the sentence:

> BEING VERB: Linda *was* the winner of the raffle.
> ACTIVE VERB: Linda *won* the raffle.

Here the verb *won* has been extracted from the noun *winner*.

Active verbs may also be extracted from adjectives, as in:

> BEING VERB: My summer at the New Jersey shore *was* enjoyable.
> ACTIVE VERB: I *enjoyed* my summer at the New Jersey shore.

Sometimes it pays to substitute an altogether fresh verb:

BEING VERB: It *is* not easy for me to express my feelings.

ACTIVE VERB: I *find* it difficult to express my feelings.

Practice will help you purge being verbs from your sentences and thereby add vitality to whatever you write.

SINCERITY

You must choose a style and words that are appropriate to the occasion. You must never be condescending, never supercilious. Your reader will know and resent your efforts.

Viewpoint is an important consideration in choosing your words. They must be selected for the person or persons to whom you wish to picture your thoughts. When Abraham Lincoln spoke at Gettysburg, the words he chose were not for himself or the dignitaries who were present. He selected words that had meaning for the veterans of the battle who leaned on their crutches or dangled empty uniform sleeves in the November wind. He knew that among his listeners there would be mothers who had lost sons, wives who had lost husbands, and brothers who had lost brothers. These people would remember what he said because he spoke for them.

Churchill in his famous "Blood, Sweat, and Tears" speech did not choose his words for the members of Parliament. He chose them for the thousands of Britishers who would bleed and sweat, and bleed and sweat some more, in the impending holocaust.

There are a number of questions you should ask yourself in order to insure the point of view of the audience with whom you wish to communicate.

1. What words will they clearly understand?
2. What would they really like to hear?
3. What are their interests?
   But far more significant,
4. What are their needs?

Having answered these questions, the point of view must be extended generally to respect the hearer's or reader's own self-respect regarding his or her abilities. Most people consider themselves capable of observing and assessing human nature, and having a capacity for imagination, broadened vision, adaptability to new ideas, and sympathetic understanding.

ORDER

The fourth part of style is order; logic must prevail. Think before you write. Make an outline, examine it, rearrange the parts to make the sequence of ideas logical, and then write. Write using parallelism, both in structure and in meaning. Avoid such a blunder as this:

> The football team wore white jerseys with blue numbers and gray helmets.

To create order and clarity, change the sentence by making the clauses parallel.

> The football team wore white jerseys with blue numbers and wore gray helmets.

or

> The football team wore both gray helmets and white jerseys with blue numbers.

When you write, also keep focus in mind. Make your topic sentence clear in the paragraph, and make every sentence in the paragraph have the same subject. If you are able to write logically, with parallelism, and with focus, you will create tightly knit paragraphs.

SELECTION OF BEST WORDS

Diction, the name given to choice of words, demands a special concern for concreteness in words. We might have many favorite abstract words—decadence, prosperity, patience, charity, temptation. But if solid nouns and verbs can make an exact word picture, naming the subject and action of decay, or of prosperity, or of patience, then pleasant generalizations and abstractions must be passed over for the sake of clarity.

Stonemasons would give little care to their choice of stones if they cared nothing about the pattern and the looks of their walls. The hardest part of building the wall is choosing the correct stones. Expressing your thoughts accurately is hard work, and finding the correct concrete word is the hardest part of all.

Generalization is soft, subject to misinterpretation, and sometimes popular, because it can be adapted to compromise. Concreteness is solid, totally devoid of vagueness, and graphically natural, because of its precision. Forceful or weak will be the judgment passed upon the words you use; and the essential element from which this judgment will be made is concreteness.

Concrete words need few modifiers. Care should be taken to avoid the use of overworked adjectives. If an adjective is used at all, it should be tested for efficiency: Is it the right adjective, or is there a brighter, better one? The same judgment must be made of adverbs, for nothing can muddle a word picture as quickly as "excess baggage" adverbs. If the verb is strong, the contribution of the adverb must be studied carefully before it is added. If the horse *galloped* over the pasture, to add that it galloped *rapidly* is questionable. The adverb modifying the adjective must also be studied with a critical eye. If the adjective had already put the icing on the cake, further icing or decoration might result in ostentation and gaudiness, reflecting only poor taste and contributing only to confusion. Form the habit of choosing among several synonyms to provide more exact modifiers when modifiers are necessary.

COMMON USAGE ERRORS

There is a subtle distinction between conversation and writing. When you speak, you are present and can clarify any errors of misunderstanding by explaining further. Consequently, oral speech need not be as precise as written work. When you write, your words must bear the burden of conveying meaning all by themselves and so must be clear and follow accepted usage.

The onslaught of television, sports announcing, and advertising, because they emphasize immediacy at the expense of depth of understanding and clarity, have blurred many of the lines between standard and nonstandard English usage.

Many usage errors arise from lack of precision. We are content to use words without knowing clearly what they mean. We also use many words when few will suffice. Taking the time and effort to be careful with your words will improve your writing and your grades.

What follows is a selected group of common usage

errors. Study them to see whether you ever commit any of them. Then work to avoid them. In so doing, you will raise your level of understanding of your language, and you will begin to develop an ear for correct grammar and diction.

Errors of Grammar

➤ Use verbal nouns (gerunds) with the possessive case rather than the participle with the obective case.

> CORRECT: I knew about *his taking* first place.
> INCORRECT: I knew about *him taking* first place.

➤ Avoid using nouns as direct modifiers.

> CORRECT: an aggressive man
> INCORRECT: an aggressive-type man

To modify one noun by another, put the modifier in a prepositional phrase.

> CORRECT: an audit *of taxes by the I.R.S.*
> INCORRECT: an I.R.S. tax audit

➤ Avoid using a negative with the word *hardly*.
Hardly means barely able, or not able. Thus, if you use a negative with it, you will be saying the opposite of what you mean.
  To say, "The boy can't hardly climb the tree," doesn't mean that the boy is barely able to climb the tree. It means that he can climb it easily. Look at it this way: The boy cannot (hardly, not able to) climb the tree. The two negatives in a row cancel one another out.

➤ Do not use the intensive pronoun as a substitute for the pronoun. Any intensive pronoun should only be used to make a noun or another pronoun stand out in the sentence.

CORRECT: St. Paul himself wrote these words.
(The word *himself* is intensifying the use of St. Paul.)

CORRECT: Martha, Mary, and I went to Washington.

INCORRECT: Martha, Mary, and myself went to Washington for the inaugural celebration.
(The word *myself* has nothing to intensify.)

➤ Do not use the word *that* after the word *but*.

CORRECT: I do not doubt *that* Henry will become a great teacher.

INCORRECT: I do not doubt *but that* Henry will become a great teacher.

CORRECT: He would have been on time, *but* he *got* stuck in traffic.

INCORRECT: He would have been on time *but that* he got stuck in traffic.

➤ Do not use the pronoun *they* without clearly indicating the antecedent. To use *they* in a nonspecific way is to betray fuzzy thinking; and certainly, it is not clear speaking.

INCORRECT: I went to the infirmary, and *they* said I had the flu.

INCORRECT: *They* say that the Infiniti is the finest car on the road today.

Who are they? The antecedents in these sentences are not expressed. No one knows who *they* are, and no one has any way of finding out.

CORRECT: I went to the infirmary, and *the nurse* said I had the flu.

CORRECT: *All my friends* say that the Infiniti is the
                 finest car on the road today.

Never, never use *they,* alone. Always make sure there
are nouns in your sentence or paragraph to explain who
they are.

Errors of Weakness

➤ Do not make nouns into verbs.

WEAK: The President will deplane in a half an hour.
STRONG: The President will leave the plane in half an
               hour.

➤ Avoid redundancies which, although correct grammati-
cally, add nothing new to the sentence.

WEAK: He is a *man who is* too fat.
STRONG: He is too fat.

➤ Avoid tautologies, the needless repetition of ideas.

   reiterate again

Reiterate means *repeat and repeat and repeat some
more.* To use the word *again* after reiterate is to write a
tautology.

   true facts

Facts can only be true, otherwise they are not facts at
all.

   *In my mind I think Michael Jordan is a great
   basketball player.*

Where else but in one's mind does one think?

➤ Do not modify the word *unique.*

Unique means *singular, one of a kind.* So to say that someone is *very unique* is to say that he or she is *very one-of-a-kind.* How can anyone be *very one,* or *more one*, or *less one*? One can only be one. Use *unique* without any modifier.

Misuse of Words

➤ can, may
Can means *be able to*.

> He *can* climb the mountain.

May means *be permitted to.*

> He *may* keep the book if he likes it.

➤ disinterested, uninterested
Disinterested means *impartial.*

> Lawyers strive to find *disinterested* jurors.

Uninterested means *lacking in interest.*

> Television commercials try to persuade *uninterested* viewers to buy new cars.

➤ effect, affect
The prefixes give the clue here. *Ef* means *from*, *af* means *toward*; so *effect* describes something that comes out of a situation, and *affect* describes something that comes to a situation.

Effect, as a noun, is the result (what came out) of an action; and as a verb, it means to produce the result.

> The elements of careful design combined for a stunning *effect* when the curtain rose on the first act.

Affect is a verb meaning to influence.

How did your training *affect* your playing?

➤ farther, further
Both declare that something has advanced.
Nonetheless, they are not interchangeable.

- *Farther* is used for distance in air, on land, or at sea.

  The sloop is *farther* out in the bay than the launch.

- *Further* is used for distance in time.

  The scientist engaged in *further* study.

➤ imply, infer
Imply means *to express indirectly.*

The reporter *implied* that the mayor was corrupt.

Infer means *to draw a conclusion.*

What can you *infer* from her choice of words?

➤ like, as
These two words are misused more often than any others. Never use them interchangeably. To keep them straight, remember how they are used.

- *Like* is a preposition and will modify nouns and is never used in verbal expressions. It means *similar to.*

  She is *like* my sister.

- *As* is a conjunction or adverb and should be used with verbs or phrases. It means, when used as an adverb, *equally, when,* or *where.*

  He is *as* tall *as* my brother.

When used as a conjunction the word *as* means *because, since,* or *in the way or manner that.*

> *As* you are going to town anyway, will you post this letter for me?
> Do *as* I say, not *as* I do.

➤ less, fewer
Both declare that something has been reduced in quantity. Nonetheless, they should not be used interchangeably.

— *Less* should only be used with abstractions or singular nouns of quantity.

> Because of my illness, I have *less* time to complete my research paper.
> Put *less* milk on my cereal next time.

— *Fewer* should only be used with numbers or concrete nouns.

> This flock has *fewer* sheep than that flock.

➤ loan, lend

— *Loan* is a noun.

> One goes to a bank to seek a *loan.*

— *Lend* is a verb.

> It is improper to say Please *loan* me some money.
> It is proper to say, Please *lend* me some money.

➤ there, their

— *There* is an adverb or is an expletive.

> *(adverb)* Look over *there.*
> *(expletive) There* are many errors of usage.

— *Their* is a possessive.

The boys said that *their* brother had won the bicycle race.

➤ *Transpire* is used incorrectly as a substitute for *occurred*. It means to *become known*, not *to happen*.

INCORRECT: The lawyer asked the witness what had *transpired*.

CORRECT: The lawyer asked the witness what had *occurred*.

➤ two, to, too

— *Two* is a number.

There are *two* books on the table.

— *To* is a preposition or a particle indicating an infinitive.

(preposition) Mary ran *to* the car.
(particle) It is difficult *to* run twenty-six miles without stopping.

— *Too* is an adverb.

The boy was *too* large to sit on the high chair.

Misuse of Prepositions

➤ Avoid the phrase *kind of* when you mean *rather*.

INCORRECT: She was *kind of* pretty.
CORRECT: She was *rather* pretty.

➤ Remember that *of* is a preposition, while *have* is a verb.

INCORRECT: He would *of* been on time, had he started earlier.

CORRECT: He would *have* been on time, had he
started earlier.

➤ *Due to* has come to mean *because* rather than an
expression to indicate something owed. When you
mean to say *because,* say so, by using *because.*

Homage is *due* a king.
The steeplechase was cancelled *because* the track
was muddy.

➤ *Inside of*—do not use *of. Inside* is complete by itself.

➤ *Later on*—do not use *on. Later* is complete by itself.

➤ *Off of*—do not use *of. Off* is complete by itself.

➤ *Plan on*—do not use *on. Plan* is complete by itself.

➤ *Subsequent to*—why use two words when one will do?
When you mean *after,* use the word itself; say *after,* not
subsequent to.

➤ *Prior to*—again, why use two words? When you mean
before, say so; use *before,* do not use *prior to.*

➤ *Words with prefixes.* When using words that have prefixes, use the English preposition that has a meaning
similar to the prefix.
According to (ac = to) is much more concise than *in
accordance with* and so is preferable.

➤ different than, different from
Different from (dif = from) is the only proper construction. *Different than* is simply wrong; *than* is not a
preposition; it is used to indicate the second of two
parts in a comparison and must follow an adjective in
the comparative degree.

Suzy is *different from* Cathy.

Suzy is *taller than* Cathy. (Note the adjective in the comparative degree, *taller,* and that Cathy is the second of two parts of a comparison.)

Barbarisms

Barbarisms are those words that have crept into our language and insidiously eaten away at clarity and forceful speech. Excise them from your everyday language and from your prose.

➤ Irregardless

Irregardless is a redundancy that betrays incompetence in language and lack of care.

Regardless means *without concern.* Adding the prefix *ir,* which means *not* or *without,* makes the word mean *not without concern*—the opposite of what you are trying to say.

➤ Enthuse

Enthuse is a verb that has sprung from a noun. Such creation of verbs is weak and ultimately shows that the speaker lacks precision.

DO NOT SAY: Edith was *enthused* about her recent trip to Europe.

SAY INSTEAD: Edith was *pleased*, or Edith was *happy*, or Edith was *enthusiastic*, about her trip.

➤ -ize or -ness words

Avoid turning words into nouns by adding the suffixes *-ize* or *-ness.*

Examples: (*-ness*) These suffixes betray a lack of *specificness* in language.

(*-ize*) *Finalize* your plans, at this point in time, to rid yourself vocabularywise of such barbarisms.

Almost any word that contains these suffixes can be replaced by a much stronger word.

Do not use *prioritize,* use instead *assign priorities.*
Do not use *finalize,* use instead *finish.*
Do not use *humbleness,* use instead *humility.*
Do not use *speediness,* use instead *speed.*

➤ -wise words
Also avoid turning adjectives into adverbs by adding the suffix *-wise.* In general, you can better express your idea by a prepositional phrase.

Do not use *contrarywise,* use instead *on the contrary.*
Do not use *likewise,* use instead *in a similar way.*

LOOKING BACK

1. The primary elements of a good writing style are emphasized in this chapter. The first one is obvious: *clarity.* What are the other three that were mentioned?

   Of the four qualities, which one could you neglect and still be considered a good writer?

2. Explain the difference between *denotation* and *connotation.* Give examples in support of your explanation.

   How many connoted meanings can you list for *light, free, head*?

   Look back at the fourteen different sentences that contain some form of *run.* Do the same for the word *sink.*

3. Which of the following sentences is correct?
   a. Sylvia can't hardly play the piano.
   b. I would of passed the test if I had been present.
   c. We returned back to the beach after lunch.
   d. How will the election affect the stock market?
   e. Alyse has less subjects than her twin sister, Gail.

If any sentences are wrong, how would you correct them?

Chapter 13
....
Research Papers: Steps to Success

TRUE CONFESSIONS

1. You are asked to do a research paper (about ten pages, or 3500 to 4000 words) for your English class on some phase of Shakespeare's life or his works. How does the assignment grab you? How will you proceed to select your topic·and begin the research?

2. The assignment for the paper on Shakespeare is given to you the third week in September. The final draft of the paper, submitted typed and in accord with the guidelines of the Modern Language Association (MLA), is due the first week of December. What kind of schedule would you prepare to enable you to get the work done on time?

3. As you proceed with your research, you find the following two footnotes in a library book. Can you explain all the information the notes contain?

---

[1]George Fischer, *Shakespeare's Education* (Bellmore, New York: Ellis & Sloane, 1972), 71.
[2]Ibid., 75.

WHAT IS A RESEARCH PAPER?

A research paper is an opportunity for you to show several things:

1. that you have thought and read about a topic on which you have become something of an authority
2. that you can use tools and methods of research
3. that you know your way around a library
4. that you can organize a bulk of information in a clear and logical way
5. that you can write in a way that makes your text interesting, informative and correct.

Basically, then, a research paper gives you the opportunity to show how good a student you are. Try to approach the task of writing one positively, not with the attitude that a research paper is just another pointless and burdensome trial that students must endure in order to get through school.

THE PROBLEM OF PLAGIARISM

When you are doing a research paper, you will be reading books and articles written by others about your topic. You will be tempted to use their knowledge as if it were your own. If you do, you may be guilty of plagiarism.

Plagiarism is the taking of someone else's words or ideas and presenting them as your own. Thus, plagiarism is fundamentally dishonest, it is a kind of thievery. Students who are idea-thieves are going on record as cheaters who cannot think for themselves and will receive the low grade they deserve.

It is inevitable, however, that you will use the ideas that others have thought about your topic. The way to do so honestly, avoiding plagiarism, is to tell your readers who created the ideas you are using. The way to tell your readers is to give credit to the authors or other sources whose ideas you have used. Later in this chapter you will find information on the form to use in acknowledging your sources.

STEPS IN WRITING A RESEARCH PAPER

Like other jobs you do as a student, the task of writing a research paper can be broken down into several steps. What follows is an organizational plan, not meant as the last word on how to do the job correctly but rather as a guide to follow while you write your paper. Thousands of students have used this plan successfully. It isn't the only plan that exists, but experience shows that it is assuredly one that works. Although the steps are listed in the order that they logically occur, the lines between them are often blurry. It's often hard to tell where one step ends and the next begins because in a complex process such as this one several steps may be occurring simultaneously.

1. The first step is to read general literature about the subject area you have chosen. It may seem strange to begin reading before you have chosen a topic, but you will find that by reading in general literature, you will be able to choose a specific topic that interests you and for which there is sufficient information to do a paper.

    In order to read in general literature, you must have an idea about your topic. For example, if you have received an assignment in history to write a paper on something that happened in the years from 1609 to 1865, you should think about what era you want to examine. Would it be the Puritans, the Revolution, the War of 1812, or the writing of the Constitution? Then, once you have chosen the general area, you would go to the reference section of your library and read articles in the encyclopedias and specialized reference works dealing with U.S. history, such as *Dictionary of American Biography.* You could also read sections of a standard textbook of U.S. history, and check your library's databases for articles and texts on each era you are thinking about as a focus for the paper.

2. As you do your reading in general literature, you should be looking for a suitable topic. Finding your topic is the second step in writing a paper.

   After you have chosen your topic, limit it. Think about what particular aspect of it you are going to examine. For example, if you decided to do research on the writing of the U.S. Constitution, you could limit your topic to "the role of James Madison in the writing of the Constitution," or "the seventeenth century political philosophers who influenced the writers of the Constitution," or perhaps "the role of Benjamin Franklin in the writing of the Constitu- tion. " By limiting your topic, you are making it specific. You will be able to guide your research and avoid reading works that pertain to your general area of research, but not to your specific topic. This limiting of your topic will become a great time saver.

3. Once you have narrowed your topic, you should begin thinking about a tentative thesis for your paper. That is, ask yourself what point you want to make about your topic. What is it that you hope to demonstrate or conclude about your topic? Say, for instance that you have discovered in your reading that James Madison not only worked hard on writing the Constitution, but that many of his personal

interests and biases are clearly reflected in its wording and substance. In other words, Madison may well be regarded as the architect of the Constitution. That idea is perfect for a thesis, for it's an idea that can be proven or demonstrated in a relatively short research paper. With a tentative thesis in mind, you can focus your reading and research directly on matters that pertain to what you are going to write in your paper. Since you know just what you are looking for, you can avoid considerable reading that is unrelated or only marginally relevant to your paper.

4. Now is the time to begin creating bibliography cards on the books, articles, and other resources you find. Use 3 × 5 index cards, one source per card.

To find book titles, use all the resources your library has to offer. Turn first to the card catalogue (if your library still has one), then to the computerized catalogue, which will list and probably print out the names of many books that are related to your topic. Encyclopedia articles will recommend books to read for further study; indexes, such as the *Reader's Guide to Periodical Literature,* will also provide help. Even if your school or town library doesn't own a particular title that looks promising, inter-library loans can be arranged. In other words, your library is likely to be connected electronically to a central catalogue of books available in school, public, and college libraries in your area. This service enables you to borrow books from any library on the network, either by going directly to the library that owns the book or by requesting the title to be sent to your own library. Obviously, the latter method is easier, but it takes considerably more time—a reason to get started on your research long before the paper is due.

Your library may also be linked to computerized databases that offer the full or the partial text of articles on many different topics. To draw on a wealth of information of this kind, you'll need to know a few basic computer search techniques. Since each system is different, you should ask your reference librarian for help.

However you obtain sources for your paper, whenever you have found a likely book, article or other resource, write down complete information on your index card. For a book put the full name of the author, the full title (including subtitle), the name of the publisher, the place of publication, and the copyright date. For articles, write the name of the author (if given), title of the article (if given), the name of the magazine or encyclopedia, the date of issue of the particular magazine or encyclopedia, and the page numbers of the article. If you are reading an encyclopedia article, include all the publishing information that you would include for any book.

Bibliography cards should contain all the information you'll need when writing footnotes in your paper or when you prepare a list of the works you cited. Having complete information at your fingertips could also be helpful in the event you need to refer to the book or resource again once you have returned it to the library. If you have gathered material with a computer and need to retrieve it, you will be greatly aided by having a record of the commands you used and the path you followed to access it the first time.

5. The next step in the process of writing a research paper is to write a working outline. A working outline is a preliminary organizer for your research. You will make your thesis statement, saying what it is that you will try to prove, and then divide your topic into its natural, general divisions. You will not need to make this outline detailed—merely a statement of what the major areas of the topic are. For example, to continue, let's see what a preliminary outline might be for the topic, "The role of James Madison in writing the Constitution."

I. Thesis statement: Madison the "architect" of our Constitution

II. Early Life
   A. Childhood, adolescence, things Madison studied
   B. What Madison did during the Revolution

III. How the Constitution was written
   A. Nature of government under "Articles of Confederation"; failure of that government
   B. Convening of the Constitutional Convention
   C. How the convention operated
      1. Factions
         a. Supporters of "Articles"
         b. "Federalists"
      2. Major ideas that were proposed

IV. Role of Madison
   A. His faction
   B. Importance to that faction
   C. His accomplishments
      1. When Convention opened
      2. As the Federalists' proposals came forth

  D. Madison's proposals

 V. Final form of Constitution.
  A. Brief survey of theoretical model of U.S.
    Government
  B. Madison's contribution

VI. Conclusion showing that thesis statement is proved

6. The sixth step is to read the works and take notes.
  Take your notes on 5 × 8 or 4 × 6 cards, one note to
  a card. Write only on one side of the card. If your
  note runs over one card, write on a second card
  rather than on the back of the first card. That way,
  when you lay the cards on your desk as you write,
  you won't have to turn them over to see what is on
  the back, and you will save time.

   At the top of each card write an abbreviation of
  the title of the work cited and the pages in the work
  from which the note came. Write down direct
  quotations if you must, but it is better to put the
  notes in your own words. Keep your cards in a box
  or packet—don't lose them.

7. After you have taken your notes, write a detailed
  outline of your paper. This outline is the one from
  which you will write your paper, so make it as
  detailed as you can. Make the arrangement of your
  ideas clear and logical.

8. Then assemble your note cards, putting them in the
  order of your final outline, and begin to write your
  first draft.

   Although each topic requires a different paper,
  the following plan, or map, explains the order of
  material and roughly how much space to devote to
  each major segment of your paper. Again, these are

guidelines only, not to be followed religiously. Your topic and good common sense should determine the proportions to use in your own paper.

A. **Introduction** (approximately 10 percent of the total paper) contains material that
   1) engages the reader's interest in the topic. Use an interesting fact or two, an unusual story, a startling statistic, an appealing anecdote—anything that will grab your reader.
   2) introduces the topic, perhaps by stating its importance or implications, its timeliness, its impact, a controversy surrounding it, or anything else that may explain why the topic is worth reading about.
   3) summarizes or states the thesis that you are trying to prove or demonstrate.

B. **Background** (approximately 20 percent), if appropriate for your topic, contains material that
   1) provides a concise history of the topic.
   2) explains key events, key people, terminology, unusual or ambiguous words or phrases in your thesis.
   3) defines the limits of time, place, scope of your paper.

C. **Main body** (approximately 40–60 percent) contains material that
   1) states important information and key evidence in support of your thesis. Use your own words. Use quotations from your sources only to support or illustrate ideas you have stated in your own words first.
   2) is organized in a sensible way. Present your arguments in order from strongest to weakest,

from least controversial to most controversial,
or in 2, 3, 1 order (that is, second best
argument, third best argument, best
argument). Think out the best order for your
particular topic and thesis.

D. **Refutation of opposition and/or reinforcement
of your position** (10–20 percent) contains
material that

   1) states other theories or opposing viewpoints,
   if any.

   2) assesses the strength of opposing arguments
   and finds their flaws.

   3) shows the strength of your ideas in
   comparison to the ideas of others.

E. **Conclusion** (10 percent) contains material that

   1) reviews your thesis, if appropriate, and your
   best reasons for its validity. Try not to rehash
   everything you've already written. Hit the
   highlights, using different wording than you
   used earlier, although you might use some of
   the same key words to remind the reader of
   what you stated before.

   2) avoids introducing new ideas that might need
   more development than you can provide in the
   conclusion.

   3) suggests that your discussion has significance
   or interest or implications beyond itself. In
   other words, indicate that there's more to be
   said and thought about your topic. Or tell the
   reader that this paper sheds light or raises
   questions about related areas of inquiry.

F. **List of works cited** (about a page) that contains
complete information about each source.

9. After you have completed a rough draft, let it cool for several days, if possible. Then return to it and reread it with an eye toward making plenty of revisions. Let others—a trusted friend, a teacher, a parent—critique your paper too. Don't be offended if they criticize; they are only trying to help. But don't immediately accept or reject what they tell you. Just ponder it, and if you think their comments are valid, make the changes they suggest. As the author of your paper, you must have the final say. Don't be pressured to make changes unless you fully agree that the changes are for the better.

10. Finally, put your paper in the form required by your teacher or school. Use a recommended system of footnoting and bibliography. If no guidelines are given, use the system suggested by the MLA (Modern Language Association) that appears later in this chapter.

PROCEEDING TO DO RESEARCH

The first thing you should do when assigned a research paper is to write down a schedule. Allot time to each of the ten steps, allowing about $1/3$ of the total time for Steps 1–4, about $1/3$ for reading and taking notes, and the remaining third for composing the paper, Steps 7–10.

To allot time to the steps, start your estimates from the date the paper is due and work backwards. For example, you have received an assignment from your history teacher and have been told that the research paper must be turned in on the last day of the term, nine weeks later.

Write a schedule like the one below, and put the date the paper is due next to Step 10. Then, next to Step 6, put the date of the day that is three weeks before the end of the term. Then, next to Step 5, put the date of the day that is six weeks before the end of the term.

After you have divided the available time into the major parts, subdivide the major areas. In our example you were given nine weeks to complete the assignment. Your division would be something like this: Of the three weeks for Steps 1–4, allow yourself about five days for general reading, about two days for selecting and limiting your topic, and about two weeks for deciding on a tentative thesis, and collecting your working bibliography; of the three weeks you allow yourself for writing, estimate that your outline will take five days, composing the rough draft about five days, revising about six days, and preparing the final copy about five days.

Once your schedule is in place, you are ready to begin. As you search through general literature, be systematic in your efforts. Being systematic is perhaps the key to success in doing research. Look carefully at all available general literature. and then when you begin to collect your bibliography, be systematic in the writing of the cards. When you are writing your notes, be systematic again. Make sure every notation is *clear,* especially the page numbers, so that you will not have to retrace your steps and redo some research because you couldn't remember from which source a good idea came.

Date Due	Step Number	Description of Step	Check Mark to Show Step Done
	1	Read in general lit.	
	2	Select & limit topic	
	3	Decide on a tentative thesis	
	4	Collect working bibliography	
	5	Write a working outline	
	6	Read and take notes	
	7	Write detailed outline	
	8	Write rough draft	
	9	Revise, revise, and revise	
	10	Put final draft in required form	

DOCUMENTING YOUR SOURCES

You must cite the source of quotations that you use in your paper. You must also give the source of ideas and opinions that you have borrowed, paraphrased, or adapted from others. Otherwise you are being academically dishonest. Basic factual material that is commonly known or is easily found in a reference book or other source does not require a citation.

Give the sources for quotations and the ideas you use in proper form. Footnotes or endnotes have been the standard for a long time, but current practice calls for sources to be documented within the text of the

paper by a brief parenthetical reference, like this:
(Trimmer 1), which means that the quote or idea comes
from page 1 of a work by someone named Trimmer. To
find more details, you would turn to the List of Works
Cited at the end of the paper, where complete bibliogra-
phical information should be given.[1]

Citations should always be as concise and clear as
possible. How to document every type of source is
beyond the scope of this book, but here are a few
examples of common citations:

➤ In parentheses, cite the author's last name and page
number:

> One writer argues that "some children may be better
> off if they escape their parents' grip, healthier if they
> grow up wild and free and sort things out on their
> own" (Denby 56).

Notice that there is no punctuation needed between
the author's name and the page number.

➤ If you name the author in your text, there is no need to
repeat the name in the citation:

> Commentator David Denby argues that "some
> children may be better off if they escape their
> parents' grip, healthier if they grow up wild and free
> and sort things out on their own" (56).

➤ If you are citing the entire work, give the author's name
in your text, but do not cite a page number:

> In a *New Yorker* article, Denby argues that parents
> cannot control their childrens' TV viewing habits, with
> or without the V-chip, so why bother to try?

---

[1]This material on documentation is adapted from Joseph F. Trimmer,
A Guide to MLA Documentation (Boston: Houghton Mifflin, 1996).

➤ If the work you are citing was written by more than one author, use only the first author's name and add *et al.,* meaning "and others." For example: (Wood, et al. 150).

➤ If the author has more than one work in your List of Works Cited, add a shortened version of the title you are referring to: For example: (Toffler, *Greening* 35*)*.

➤ If no author is given, cite the work by the first word or words of the title: ("Living with Deer" 12).

All your citations should refer to items listed alphabetically in your List of Works Cited at the end of your research paper. By turning to your list readers should readily find complete information about the book, article, pamphlet or other source that you used. This gives readers a chance to pursue the topic in greater depth, if they are so inclined, and it also allows them to judge the validity of the information in your paper. If, for example, you claimed in your paper that Great Britain's royal family is free of marital strife, the copyright date of the book—say, 1960—would instantly show that the assertion is out of date.

Therefore, you should take pains to prepare an accurate and thorough List of Works Cited. As the title suggests, the list contains only those works you have actually made reference to in your paper. Your teacher may prefer that you prepare a list of works consulted, however, in which case you need to keep track of every work that you used, whether or not you referred to it. The term *bibliography,* meaning list of books, is no longer applicable in many research papers because modern students often use films, CD-ROMS, interviews, newspaper articles and other non-book sources.

Use the following guidelines, recommended by the MLA, to set up your list.

1. The list should come immediately after the last page of your paper. Number the page accordingly.
2. Double space all items on the list. Use indentations as illustrated in the examples shown below.
3. List items in alphabetical order according to the last name of the author. If the work has more than one author, use the name of the first one listed. If no author is indicated, alphabetize according to the title of the work, excluding words like *a, an,* and *the.*
4. Underline or *italicize* the titles of books, plays, films, CD's, videos, magazines, and pamphlets.
5. Put quotation marks around the names of short stories, essays, articles, editorials, poems, chapter titles, songs, lectures, and any unpublished material.
6. Use a period and a space to separate the author (last name first), the title, and the publication information.

Examples of items frequently found in a list of works:

➤ If a book has one author:

> MacLean, Norman. <u>Young Men and Fire</u>. Chicago: University of Chicago Press, 1992.

➤ If you are citing two different works by the same author:

> Abbey, Edward. <u>Confessions of a Barbarian</u>. Boston: Little Brown, 1994.
> _____ <u>Fire on the Mountain</u>. Albuquerque: University of New Mexico Press, 1962.

➤ If a book has more than one author:

> Edwards, Paul, and Arthur Pap. <u>Modern Introduction to Philosophy</u>. New York: The Free Press, 1965.

➤ If no author is given:

> <u>Town of Harrison Tricentennial</u>. Charles Dawson
>   History Center, 1996.

➤ If an editor but no author is given:

> Zinsser, William, ed. <u>Inventing the Truth: The Art</u>
>   <u>and Craft of Memoir</u>. Boston: Houghton Mifflin,
>   1987.

➤ If an article with author's name appears in a periodical
or newspaper:

> Cantwell, Mary. "How to Make a Corpse Talk." <u>New</u>
>   <u>York Times Magazine</u> 14 July 1996: 14-17.

➤ If an unsigned article appears in a periodical or newspaper:

> "Teenagers Meet the Elderly," <u>Practice Digest</u> 3:1
>   (June 1980): 23-24.

➤ If you use a CD-ROM:

> <u>Picture Atlas of the World</u>. CD-ROM. National
>   Geographic, 1994.

➤ If you use a source from a computer network:

> Altman, Gary. "Olympic Madness." AOL. World
>   Wide Web. 8 July 1996.

➤ If you use a film:

> <u>Courage Under Fire</u>. Dir. Edward Zwick. With
>   Denzel Washington and Meg Ryan. 20th
>   Century Fox, 1996.

Preparing a list of works can sometimes be frustrat-
ing and time consuming. Doing it perfectly, though, is
a signal to your reader (presumably your teacher) that
you respect the established practices of academic

scholarship. You are bound to be rewarded for the effort, both in the pride you'll feel about doing it right and in the grade you earn for the paper.

THE GRADE YOU EARN

If you look on the research paper as a challenge and a chance for discovery and creative work, the product will be what you'd expect—a well-written piece of work, reflecting wide reading and a firm grasp of material. Your teacher will be intellectually stimulated while reading it and will reward you with the grade you deserve.

Originality in the term paper is always of great value, but your grade probably is derived more from the scope of the paper—scope referring to the extent of the writer's reading on the subject before he or she starts to write. Originality, like all other inventiveness, is not the gift of all, but there is no student who cannot read widely and fulfill the basic obligation of having a good working knowledge of the subject. Only by doing the extensive study first does the writer ever arrive at the place where the imaginative consideration of the ideas of others may bring into existence new ideas.

PRACTICES FOR BETTER RESEARCH PAPERS

➤ Make a schedule of the ten steps in research and assign a date for completion of each step. Put the schedule in your work place.

➤ Allow $^1/_3$ of your allotted time for writing.

➤ Use all of the resources of your library, including the librarian.

➤ If you find you have chosen a topic for which you can't gain ready access to information, *change your topic,* and revise your work schedule. You should be able to tell whether you need to change when you try to compile your working bibliography. If you can't find many books and articles, take the hint—you will have a difficult time gathering notes and writing your paper.

➤ Be systematic in taking your notes. Make sure that every page number is accurate and that you will be able to find the passage cited if you are asked to do so.

LOOKING BACK

1. Why is it important for a footnote to contain the publication date of a book? Why the place of publication?

   CLUES: Suppose it were a book on physics or one on economics.

2. "The ten research steps are very comprehensive," said Josh, "but as I see it, unless you pick the right topic, you are in deep trouble."

   What's your reaction to Josh's statement? Is selection of the right topic the most important of all the steps? Why?

3. Let us suppose that you selected "Shakespeare and Religion" as your topic. You scour the public library and your school's library, but find only two brief references to the topic. *The Encyclopedia Britannica* provides you with a few additional notes.

   You have four weeks left to complete and submit the research paper. What should you do?

Chapter 14

The Library: How to Use It

TRUE CONFESSIONS

1. In your opinion, what is the most important space in your school? The locker room? The guidance office? The library? The cafeteria?

   Although all those locations have their place in the life of a school, this chapter takes the position that the library is the heart of any academic institution, large or small. Tell why you agree or disagree.

2. Time for a true or false test:
   a. The Dewey Decimal System is especially useful for those taking algebra tests. T or F?
   b. Roget's *Thesaurus* is a beautiful sculpture of an extinct animal. T or F?
   c. *The Reader's Guide* recommends worthwhile books for high-school and college students. T or F?

   Can you explain why the answer is F to all three questions?

3. Today's libraries contain much more than books. Name at least three other kinds of materials you are likely to find there.

HOW TO FIND A BOOK

Chapter 4 suggested that libraries provide both atmosphere and incentive for serious study, and that if you do not have satisfactory conditions at home, the library habit could become one of your best study habits. The most important room or building at your school and in your town or city is perhaps the library. The purpose of this chapter is to prepare you to find what you want in the library and make known to you what is available there.

A state-of-the art library contains an awesome array of print and non-print materials. But the foundation of any library, however well-stocked and technologically up-to-date it may be, is still the trusty, old-fashioned book—that thing with pages, print, and a hard cover.

To find a book that your library owns, it helps to know the name of the author, a key word in the title, or the main subject matter. With this information you are prepared to search for the book, either in the card catalogue or in the computer catalogue of the library's holdings.

The card catalogue, if your library still uses one, is contained in a series of drawers labeled with the letters of the alphabet. The cards inside really make up an alphabetical index to the library and are filed alpha-betically by author's last name, by book title (beginning with the first important word—not *A, An,* or *The*)—and by subject. The *title card* is probably the quickest one to find if you know what book you want.

EXAMPLE OF TITLE CARD

	Surviving an eating disorder	(Title)
	Seigel, Michele	(Author)
616.85Se	Oxford University Press, 1995	(Call # and publication data)

Suppose you read the book and would like to read some more of the author's work. Return to the card

catalogue and look up Seigel, Michele. If the library
owns any additional books by Michele Seigel, the
author cards will tell you their titles, dates of
publication, and so forth. There will be an author card
for each separate work by the author.

If you wish to pursue your study of eating disorders,
but don't know the authors or titles, a third card is
available to help you. It is called the *subject card,* and
will be indexed under a general subject (EATING) or
under any number of more specific or related subjects,
such as EATING DISORDERS, ANOREXIA, BULIMIA, OBESITY,
PSYCHOLOGY, and so on. Subject cards are usually not
included for works of fiction, however, so you won't
find a Stephen King novel by looking up HORROR,
MURDER, GHOSTS, DEVIL WORSHIP, CULTS, and other such
goodies.

Using the computer to search for a book is not much
different from using the card catalogue, particularly if
you know the title or author. Computer catalogues are
user-friendly and will instruct you every step of the
way. To locate a book, you simply type in answers to
the questions you see on the monitor, hit ENTER on the
keyboard, and in a moment you will know whether the
library owns the book you are looking for. Knowing
either the title of the book or the author's name ahead
of time will speed up the process.

If you use the computer to search for books on a
certain subject, you type in a key word, and the computer will quickly give you a list of titles containing
that key word. If the word you typed is fairly general,
you will probably find numerous titles that contain the
key word but have nothing to do with the subject you
have in mind. For instance, if your interest is eating
disorders, and you typed EATING in the subject box, you

would end up with a list of hundreds of titles that include cook books, diet books, books about nutrition, books on cuisines of the world, books on the history of food, and even a play called *Eating People is Wrong.* To narrow the search, type in EATING DISORDERS, a more specific subject that will generate a far shorter list. After perusing the list, which may contain a brief description of each book, you may wish to know more details about a particular title. In that case, the computer screen will display more information about the book than you need to know. Because you might need the information later, though, it may pay to copy it, either by hand or by a printer that is connected to the computer.

Title:	Straight talk about eating disorders
Author:	Maloney, Michael, 1944 -
Publisher:	New York, NY: Dell Publ., 1993, c. 1991
Collation:	138 pages; 18 cm paperback
Note:	Includes bibliographical references and index

616.85M (PBK)

In many libraries, the computer will also tell you whether the book is available or has been checked out. Should the book be out, the computer may search the collections of other libraries on the network and tell you where another copy can be found.

No doubt you have noticed that library books are also identified by numbers. These numbers are symbols in a classification system that provides you with a *call number* by which you can search for the books you want. The same number tells the librarian in what section of the library, on what shelf, and in what specific order on the shelf each book is to be found.

When you intend to seek a book from the library shelves, write down the call number, author, and title, and carry that information with you. In some college and university libraries access to the shelves, or stack as they are sometimes called, is limited to members of the staff or to researchers. To obtain a book in such libraries, you will fill out a request form and wait for a library runner to bring the book to you.

SYSTEMS OF CLASSIFICATION

There are two widely used systems of classification: the Dewey Decimal System and the Library of Congress System. The Dewey Decimal System is the one you will probably see in small public and school libraries. It was developed at Amherst College in 1873 and catalogues all knowledge under *ten divisions,* each division being assigned a group of numbers.

DEWEY DECIMAL SYSTEM

Numbers	Main Divisions	Subdivisions
000-099	General Works	Almanacs, encyclopedias, bibliographies, magazines, newspapers. Materials that cannot be narrowed to a single subject.
100-199	Philosophy	Logic, history of philosophy, systems of philosophy, ethics, and psychology.

DEWEY DECIMAL SYSTEM (*Continued*)

Numbers	Main Divisions	Subdivisions
200-299	Religion	Sacred writings (the Bible), mythology, history of religions, all religions and theologies.
300-399	Sociology (Social Sciences)	Group dynamics, law, government, education, economics.
400-499	Philology (Study of Lingustics)	Dictionaries dealing with words (not of biographies), grammars and technical studies of all languages.
500-599	Science (Subject and Theoretical)	Astronomy, biology, botany, chemistry, mathematics, physics, etc.
600-699	Applied Science (Useful Arts)	Agriculture, all types of engineering, business, home economics, medicine, nursing, etc.
700-799	Fine Arts (Professional and Recreative)	Architecture, painting, music, performing arts, sports, etc.
800-899	Literature	All types of literature— drama, essays, novels, poetry, etc.—in all languages of all countries.

DEWEY DECIMAL SYSTEM (*Continued*)

Numbers	Main Divisions	Subdivisions
900-999	History	All history, biography, geography, travel, etc.

If you go to the section of the library shelving Applied Science, 600-699, you will see immediately that each division is further divided. For example, 600-610 will have general books or collections dealing with applied science. Medicine will be classified under 610. Books on engineering will begin with 620 and be further broken down by smaller decimals. A glance at the history shelves will reveal that 900-909 are general works of history; 910 is geography; and so on by decimal subdivision. English is subdivided into literature of nations, then further catalogued. For example, English literature is 820; English poetry 821; English drama 822; and so on to 829.99. English poetry, 821, is further subdivided; 821.1 is Early English poetry; and so on to 821.9, each subdivision designating a specific period. A little observation will make it easy for you to find the exact spot in a particular section of the library where the subject you are interested in can be pinpointed.

The Library of Congress System, used primarily in research libraries, such as those found in graduate schools and universities, but rarely in high school libraries, is an alternate system that designates the main divisions of knowledge by letters instead of numbers. Subdivisions in the Library of Congress System are made by the addition of a second letter and whole numbers. Within the main divisions, books relating to a specific topic are grouped together and within these topic subdivisions, books are shelved alphabetically according to the author's name.

LIBRARY OF CONGRESS SYSTEM

Letter	Main Divisions
A	General Works
B	Philosophy and Religion
C	History—Auxiliary Sciences
D	History—Topography (except American)
E–F	American History—Topography
G	Geography—Anthropology
H	Social Sciences
J	Political Sciences
K	Law
L	Education
M	Music
N	Fine Arts
P	Language—Literature (nonfiction)
Q	Sciences
R	Medicine
S	Agriculture
T	Technology
U	Military Science
V	Naval Science
Z	Bibliography and Library Science
P–Z	Literature (fiction)

FICTION AND BIOGRAPHY

Fiction and biography may be arranged in separate sections. Libraries using the Dewey Decimal System are more likely to follow this arrangement than libraries using the Library of Congress System.

In the fiction section, the books are arranged alphabetically by the author's last name. In case of two or more books by the same author, they are shelved alphabetically by title. Some libraries use the classification symbol *F* or *Fic* plus the first letter of the author's last name.

Biography is usually classified by the letter B in libraries that use the Dewey Decimal classification. Those libraries that use the Library of Congress classification will shelve biographies with other works best reflecting the occupation of the person whose life is being narrated.

Here is a card for collective biography. Some of the information is explained below:

①
920   Rome—Biography

P   Plutarch

        Plutarch's Lives. The translation called
Dryden's. Corrected from Greek and
revised by A. H. Clough—

  ② 5 v. Boston, Little, Brown and Co. 1872

  ③ L.C. DE7. P5 1872   ④ 8–14601

① Call number
② Five volumes
③ Library of Congress Catalogue number
④ Library of Congress card number

With this information fresh in your mind, visit your school or public library. Discover the ease with which you can find your way from one section to another. When in doubt, ask the librarians. They are there to help.

REFERENCE BOOKS

Reference books provide invaluable help to the student by making important information easily accessible. That is the whole function of the reference section of the library. As you prepare themes, reports, essays, or research papers, you can help yourself get a good start by using these books. They not only will give you general information about a topic, but will direct you to other works that cover your topic in greater depth.

In addition to providing access to general information, the reference section of a library is also a microcosm of the whole library. By walking through it, you will learn how the whole library is arranged, since the reference books will be organized according to the classification system used throughout the library.

Reference sections of libraries will contain many different kinds of works, and what follows here is merely a guide to some basic kinds of reference books.

Perhaps the first book to catch your eye in the reference section of the library will be an unabridged dictionary, a book of such size that it has its own special rack. An unabridged dictionary contains nearly all the words in the language, giving definitions, showing pronunciation, and presenting information about the origin and history of each word. As well as entries about words, such a dictionary contains biographical and geographical information, abbreviations, tables of weights and measures, and commonly used foreign phrases. Two unabridged dictionaries often found are Merriam-Webster's unabridged dictionary and the Random House unabridged dictionary of the English language. The most comprehensive of all the dictionaries is the *Oxford English Dictionary*. It is many volumes long, and because of the exhaustive length and the high quality of its scholarship, it is the most respected authority on words.

In order to use these massive books, you will need to know the abbreviations the editors have used. Abbreviations and their meanings will be listed, either in the front or back. Be sure to consult this list whenever you are in doubt about the meaning of an entry.

In addition to dictionaries, reference sections of libraries may contain thesauruses of words, usually Roget's or a modernized version of this work. A thesaurus is a compilation of synonyms and so is valuable to anyone doing any kind of writing.

Another source of good information about words is *The New Century Cyclopedia of Names,* which provides an abundance of information about the origins, history, and meaning of names used in English. Two sources of information about English as spoken and written in the United States are H. L. Mencken's *The American Language* and Bergen Evans' *Dictionary of Contemporary American Usage.*

In your English class you may be asked to write essays about works of literature. The reference section of the library contains many examples of literary criticism and much information about authors. *Contemporary Literary Criticism* is a collection of reviews of books by living authors. *Twentieth Century Literary Criticism* contains biographical essays about authors, as well as collections of reviews and essays about them. *Contemporary Authors* has few reviews of works, but is filled with biographical information about living authors, including lists of titles of their written works. *Book Review Digest* is perhaps the standard reference of literary criticism, for it contains excerpts from reviews of almost all published nonfiction and fiction. Any work of nonfiction that receives two reviews in periodicals or journals will be listed and so will any work of fiction that receives four reviews.

Whenever you are asked to do a research paper, one place to look for a topic is in general encyclopedias. Encyclopedias, their very name derived from the Greek *enkyklios* (encircle) and *paideia* (education), enclose in one volume or set of volumes masses of information on nearly any conceivable topic.

Every reference section of libraries will contain encyclopedias, some libraries will have several. Most common are *World Book*, especially written for younger people, *Americana, Britannica,* and *Colliers,* but there are others as well. Most encyclopedias update their information by adding a volume, called an annual or a yearbook, each year for a decade or so after publication.

All encyclopedias are arranged alphabetically by subject, and most contain indexes both to topics and contributing authors. The essays in encyclopedias are written by experts; give information in a clear, compact form; and will often contain a brief bibliography of other works that pertain to the essay's topic.

In addition to these encyclopedias of many volumes, there is an excellent single volume work, *The Columbia Encyclopedia.* It covers the vast array of human knowledge, but necessarily devotes less space to topics than a multiple-volumed work does.

There are also specialized encyclopedias that deal with particular subjects and are limited to particular fields of knowledge such as art, science, technology, music, or history. Libraries sometimes have encyclopedias that limit their scope to particular religions and ethnic groups, such as the *Catholic Encyclopedia* or the *Jewish Encyclopedia.*

For information on contemporary events you can turn to one or another of the yearbooks that you might find in the reference section. *Facts on File* is an annual collection of digests of news articles on current events, and all subjects are indexed for easy use. Annuals, such as the *World Almanac,* contain up-to-date statistics, some valuable facts about government agencies and personnel, sports, scientific developments, and information on many other topics. Both national and state governments produce yearbooks of various kinds. You will find all of these works to be of great assistance if you have to prepare a paper on contemporary developments.

Most reference sections also contain numerous biographical dictionaries. Some volumes will be specifically devoted, for example, to musicians, writers, or statesmen. Others will give sketches of noteworthy persons from every walk of life. *Who's Who in America, Dictionary of American Biography, Webster's Biographical Dictionary,* and *Chambers's Biographical Dictionary* are general works. *Dictionary of National Biography* is devoted to noteworthy citizens of Great Britain. *Current Biography*, published in magazine form several times a year, and put in book form by years, is a place to gather facts on someone who has become prominent in the immediate present.

In addition to contemporary material afforded by yearbooks, there are many interesting and valuable articles in magazines and newspapers. *The Reader's Guide to Periodical Literature* is the standard reference to magazine articles. The *Reader's Guide* is published twice a month and lists alphabetically, by author and subject, the significant articles from more than a hundred magazines. *The New York Times Index* is a guide to the articles found in that newspaper. The Index is published in two-week increments and lists alphabetically, by subject or author, articles, editorials, book reviews, and obituaries that appear in the paper. Each article is listed giving the date, sometimes the section, page, and column of the paper in which that article appears. If you find only a listing for a date, you are being referred to another subject. Turn to that subject in the index and you will find all articles listed chronologically. That is where that mysterious date will help you find the actual citation for your article. Because libraries can't store mountains of newspapers dating back over a hundred years, articles from the *New York Times* can be found on microfilm or micro-fiche, or in some libraries on CD-ROM. The librarian will be glad to show you how to gain access to and use any of these indispensable tools.

TAPES, CD'S, AND VIDEOS

Many school and public libraries have well-stocked audiovisual departments containing audio tapes of books, music, speeches, lectures, plays, poetry, and lots more.

Thousands of books, both fiction and non-fiction, have been recorded, some of them books that you may have been assigned to read by your English or social studies teacher. You can borrow the books on tape to listen in your car, on your Walkman, or wherever you go. In addition, your library's collection of tapes may include memoirs, true-life mysteries, self-help books, books on travel, comedy, adventure, science, sports—almost anything at all. As for current popular music, you are not likely to find much of a selection in the library, but there will be plenty of tapes and CD's of classical performances, Broadway show tunes, folk songs, and a variety of other music.

Most libraries also have a videotape collection, for both education and entertainment. Because libraries don't want to compete with Blockbuster, the selection of tapes will be different from that found in your local video store, and may include anything from how to improve your tennis game to the best way to apply makeup. You'll also find videos on travel, nature, health and fitness—virtually any topic of interest. Feature films are popular, too, but the selection is likely to be made up of older, often historically significant, and foreign films.

PERIODICALS AND MICROFILM

Typically, libraries subscribe to scores, if not hundreds, of periodicals. The periodical room of many libraries is often the most crowded space in the building, attracting readers of magazines on every conceivable subject. A glance at the periodical collection in your library will reveal that you can read about airplanes, basketball, crafts, fashions, nature, movies, rock climbing, foreign policy, furniture, teen life, music, and much more.

Because so much is published, even the biggest libraries have neither the space nor the resources to store everything worth reading. As a solution to the problem, vast quantities of information have been reduced in volume and in cost by microfilms and microfiche (sometimes called microcards). Most microfilm or microfiche holdings will be of news-papers (*The New York Times*), periodicals (*Time, U.S. News and World Report*), or rare books that would be too expensive to buy, such as an early manuscript of a play by Shakespeare. As you do research for history papers or perhaps for an English assignment, you may find that the material you want to read is on microfilm. Librarians will help you find the articles you want, show you how to use the microfilm and microfiche readers, and how to make photocopies of the pages you need.

COMPUTERS

Computers in the library serve several functions. Not only do they help you locate material, but if your library is connected to any online databases, you will have access to a wealth of information that you may not be able to find inside the walls of the library. By hooking up to an electronic periodical index, you are multiplying by many times the possible sources you have available for doing your research. If, for instance, you are preparing a report on water pollution for a science or social studies class, you might tap into OPAC (Online Public Access Catalogue) or the EBSCO Magazine Index, which would give you the names of numerous articles that contain the words WATER POLLUTION somewhere in their text. To be certain that the article is germane to your interest, you might tell the computer to restrict the search to articles that contain the phrase several times or to seek out articles that also mention the Hudson River. The more limits you place on the search, the more likely you will find material you can actually use for your schoolwork.

Once you have found some promising titles, you may be able to get ABSTRACTS, or brief summaries, of each article, or depending on the sources and databases you are using, printouts of the complete texts. You should know, however, that some sources of data, such as the Electronic Library, will charge you for sending you the full text of an article. To pay for it, you need a credit card number that you would type on the computer screen.

If you know the general topic you want to pursue, your librarian can advise you on which database is most likely to serve you best and most cheaply, and can help you interpret the mass of information that you may get in response to what may seem like a simple request.

Some libraries will give you access to the Internet— sometimes for a fee, sometimes for nothing. Once online, you have the entire world at your disposal. Navigating the Internet takes time and practice, but a skillful surfer can tap the resources of universities, libraries, museums, government agencies, and countless other repositories of information.

The computers in some libraries also come equipped with CD-ROM players. Students will find a vast and varied amount of information on CD-ROM's. Much of it is similar to what is available in books, but for many students the combination of light, sound, color, and movement on CD-ROM's takes the drudgery out of the learning. Few CD-ROM's offer the depth and scope that books can offer. Using CD-ROM's is generally comparable to relying on TV news broadcasts as a sole source of information about what's going on in the world. For a solid understanding of the world's affairs and current issues, one must depend on other media. Nevertheless, CD-ROM's are here to stay and over time are likely to become more useful for the serious scholar.

It was stated at the beginning of this chapter that the library may be the most important space in your school, even the most important place in town. There is no better way to end this chapter than to state simply that tests given to both high school and college students reveal that those who make the highest marks are those who know how to use the library and use it regularly. It is a place for study, a place that provides the greatest storehouse of learning material. So learn to use it, use it to boost your grades, to widen your horizons, and enlarge your life.

PRACTICES FOR BETTER LIBRARY USE

1. Form the library habit. Get hooked.
2. Learn how to find material doing a search on the library's computer catalogue.
3. Save time by learning the locations of certain kinds of books in your library. Where, for instance, would you find a book of paintings by Winslow Homer? Where would you find the autobiography of General Colin Powell? How about a book on edible plants and roots?
4. Know the methods of arranging fiction and biography used by your library. Arrangements vary from one library to another.
5. Study the reference section to learn generally what is available, its location, and the use to which the various materials may be put.
6. Learn to make a working bibliography as you find material on the topic you are studying. For a model bibliography, check several at the end of articles in one or two encyclopedias. Use the card method (3 × 5 index cards) of making your bibliography so you can rearrange at will. Know the difference

between a working and an exhaustive bibliography
(an exhaustive bibliography lists everything ever
written on the topic). Choose a limited topic, some
significant yet not too well-known historical character, and discover the excitement and methodical
investigation involved in preparing a complete bibliography. Be sure to limit your topic—not
Financiers of the American Revolution, rather *Haym
Salomon*—not the *Mimic* (Mimidae) *Family* of
birds, rather the *Mockingbird.*

LOOKING BACK

1. Using the Dewey Decimal System, where would
   you look to find the following books?
   a. *Concepts in Modern Biology* by David Kraus
   b. *The Essential Shakespeare* by John Dover
      Wilson
   c. *Economics* by Paul A. Samuelson

2. What kind of information can we expect to find
   about words in the *Merriam Webster Unabridged
   Dictionary*?
   Use that dictionary or any other unabridged
   dictionary that is available to look up the following:
   *sleazy, cabal, Hobson's choice, narcissism,
   cyberspace.*

3. The personnel manager of a large corporation said,
   "I don't necessarily hire the most intelligent
   applicant, but I almost always go for the one who
   knows how to find the necessary information."
   What did he mean? What is the relevance of that
   personnel manager's statement to this chapter?

Chapter 15

Computers for Learning

In this technological age every student grapples with problems of increasing mechanization, not only in the society at large, but in school, too. Some schools devote considerable resources to teaching students to become competent and knowledgeable computer users. Others provide equipment but little instruction, leaving it up to the students themselves to learn about computers and how they function. With the digital age upon us, all students face the challenges of learning the use of computers, a skill that has joined the three R's as a basic aim of education. Without computer literacy, a young man or woman won't be well-prepared for participation in the society of the twenty-first century.

In 1995, Nicholas Negroponte, Professor of Media Technology at MIT, tried to describe the rapid infusion of computer technology into our daily lives: "Thirty-five percent of American families and 50 percent of American teenagers have a personal computer at home; 30 million people are estimated to be on the Internet; 65 percent of the new computers sold worldwide in 1994 were for the home; and 90 percent of those to be sold this year are expected to have modems or CD-ROM drives. . . And if I am wrong about any of the numbers above, just wait a minute." [1]

WHAT COMPUTERS CAN DO

The technological advances in computers are so rapid that books like this one cannot keep pace with the

---

[1] *Being Digital* (New York: Knopf, 1995), 5.

changes. One fact that will remain constant, however, is that computers will continue to become increasingly important in our lives. A majority of jobs require the use of computers, and no one can remain immune from their influence. Bill Gates, the head of the giant Microsoft Corporation, boasts that "we caused a kind of revolution—peaceful, mainly—and now the computer has taken up residence in our offices and homes. Computers shrank in size and grew in power, as they dropped dramatically in price. And it all happened fairly quickly. Not as quickly as I once thought, but still pretty fast. Inexpensive computer chips now show up in engines, watches, antilock brakes, facsimile machines, elevators, gasoline pumps, cameras, thermostats, treadmills, vending machines, burglar alarms, and even talking greeting cards."[2]

Computers can be a great boon to anyone's education. How will you use this remarkable and powerful tool to your advantage as a student? The remainder of this chapter is meant to give you some ideas.

Regardless of the kind of computer that is available to you—Macintosh or PC—your schoolwork is likely to engage you more fully when you use a computer regularly. Granted, you now may be able to think of a million things you'd rather do than spend time in the computer lab, but with a little patience and perseverance, you're soon apt to discover how computers can enrich your studies and improve your performance in school. In general, there are five areas in which computers can be helpful: (1) writing and editing, (2) retrieving information, (3) communicating, (4) acquiring new skills and knowledge, and (5) presenting your work.

---

[2]*The Road Ahead* (New York: Viking, 1995), 2–3.

WRITING AND EDITING

Through a word-processing program a computer can help you become a better writer very quickly. Typing skills, or keyboarding as typing has come to be known, are very important, although some people can type very rapidly using just a few fingers. Those who type the fastest, however, are those who have learned to touch-type, either by taking a typing class or by teaching themselves. (Typing software can be installed in most computers—an easy way to learn to type.) In either case, typing with fluency will enable you to rapidly put your thoughts into writing, make changes and corrections easily, and rearrange your thoughts into the best sequence. Many students find that word processing unlocks their latent talents; reluctant writers become eager to compose papers, stories, and poetry. The key that a computer provides to unlock this talent is the ease of composition and editing. Through this one aspect alone, word processing may be your most valuable computer tool.

Almost every computer sold comes with an installed word processing program. Although great numbers of programs exist, they all resemble each other and work basically the same way. Once you have mastered, say, Macwrite on the Macintosh, or WordPerfect on the PC, you will have little trouble switching between word processing programs. Some of the commands may be slightly different, and each may have features that another doesn't, but after a little while the differences become inconsequential. The more powerful programs may check your spelling and grammar, enable you to write footnotes more easily, permit you to leave space in your text for pictures and graphics, let you type in two or more columns on a page, and so forth, but even the most rudimentary programs will undoubtedly enhance your writing performance in English and other classes.

FINDING INFORMATION

It's small wonder that the present era is sometimes called the Information Age. With the advent of the computer, we have been given access to more information than we could ever want or need. The previous chapter in this book describes just a handful of possibilities for doing electronic searches for material on virtually every imaginable topic. Many libraries subscribe to information services whose sole function is to help you find whatever you may be looking for. The Internet expands still further the resources available to you. You could spend the rest of your life cruising on the Internet and never run out of places to contact for information. Not everything you find on your screen is worth the effort of the search, but very often the documents, databases, images, and even other computer software than you can load into your own computer make the time and effort very worthwhile. With a computer, a modem—the equivalent of a telephone—and some basic research software, you can literally stay at your desk while exploring the world for information.

Randy, a junior in a Washington state high school, writing about his telecommunications learning, said "The best aspect of the 'Net is the ability to get information on any topic. There are lots of ways to do this. First, you can join listserv and find out about a topic from experts. Second, you can e-mail an expert in a field with a question and get an answer to your question quickly. But the best way to get materials is through Gopherspace. I recently needed information on Poland.

I entered Gopherspace, moved to a server in Poland itself, and there I found all the information I needed on my subject. "[3]

Literally at your fingertips, you have encyclopedias, everything printed in today's newspapers, weather information, the latest stock prices, databases on science, social studies, sports, business, and on and on and on. The U.S. Congress now gives access to the full text of all House and Senate bills, including summaries and chronologies of pending legislation, as well as the text of the *Congressional Record,* which reports every word uttered in Congress and is updated daily. If you are studying a foreign language you might make contact with a site in in the country where the language is spoken. A university in France, for example, maintains a site that features pointers about traveling throughout the country, provides information about places to visit, language, food, and culture. The Internet also offers SAT and ACT preparation, virtual tours of 3,500 colleges and universities, and so on.

Having all this information readily available is one thing; how to use it to enhance your perfomance as a student is another. While some schoolteachers are attuned to technology, most are still struggling to learn the in's and out's of using computers in the curriculum. As a student, you have a grand opportunity to show your teachers how savvy you are. Use data retrieved from computer for your next report or project. Not only will you learn something of value, but your teachers are certain to be impressed. Who knows, your teachers may come to you begging for a computer lesson or two.

---

[3] *The Internet Manual for Classroom Use* (Arlington, VA: Educational Research Service, 1995), 5

COMMUNICATING

Through e-mail and chat groups, both available via the Internet, students make contact with people all over the world—other students, teachers, friends, experts in every field.

If you or your school has e-mail capability, people everywhere on the planet can participate in your education. Traditionally, teachers have encouraged students to be pen pals with students in far-off places. Through e-mail, you can easily be a key pal with anyone, young or old, famous or ordinary. Rachel, a Washington, D.C. student, wrote, "Being on a network has expanded my circle of friends. . . . When I communicate with someone in Slovenia or England or Argentina I realize that the problems that they have are not very far away from me. So even though we are all far away from each other in miles, we are all part of the same global community."[4]

Entire classes get involved in e-mail correspondence. A science class in Maine, for example, gathered and collected data on area wildlife to exchange for similar information with students in Hawaii. A New York high school class studying Russian literature became key pals with students in a school near Moscow. When it came time to write about the books they'd been reading, the American students asked their Russian counterparts to give them ideas about Tolstoy, Chekhov, and the other authors. The papers that were submitted, according to the teacher, were "the most interesting and varied" he had ever read. Through the Global Student Newswire, founded by journalism

---

[4]Ibid., 4.

students at the University of Florida, you and the editors of your school newspaper can share ideas and content for publication. Occasionally, certain celebrities go online for a period of time to talk electronically with students. Recently students made personal contact with astronauts, former presidents, well-known scholars, authors, and poets.

The Internet also allows you to join chat groups composed of people with a common interest. To be sure, much of the electronic conversation may be insipid and a waste of time, but you never know when you might find a soulmate with whom to connect. Say, for instance, you participate in a group that is chatting about a passion of yours—movies. If one of the group seems particularly well-informed or engaging, you can exchange e-mail addresses and carry on a dialogue without the interference of other, less interested participants.

How these opportunities can make a difference to your performance in school is up to you. You may not earn extra credit for using e-mail, but think how the experience can add to your fund of knowledge and the pleasure you derive from learning. Although your grade-point average may not shoot up merely because you've gone online, you will ultimately be a more well-rounded person because of your greater aware-ness of the world and the broad perspectives you have gained.

ACQUIRING NEW SKILLS AND KNOWLEDGE

The amount of study material being published for students' use is overwhelming. In every subject, from art to tech-ed, the number of computer programs being sold suggests that CAI (computer-assisted instruction) is here to stay. Some of the programs are simple and easy to use. In fact, they are little more than textbooks transferred to computer disks. If you were to use a computer program to study for SAT I, for instance, the study material might come directly from a book. The computer makes the experience interactive, however, meaning that you'll see comments about your answers flashed on the screen, and your performance level will often determine which material you'll work on next. In all, such programs create the illusion that studying is less solitary than it really is and that someone (a computer chip, perhaps) is accompanying you as you work through the program.

Other programs are more varied and creative. CSILE (computer-supported intentional learning environment), for one, offers students in two different classes, two schools, even two different countries a chance to work together. Each class invents its own hypothetical ancient culture, produces, and buries artifacts used in that culture. Then each class does an archaeological dig at the other class' site, drawing inferences about the culture from the materials they uncover. A good deal of electronic conversation occurs between the classes as they explore the food, art, religion, language, values, and other aspects of each others culture.

This kind of simulation exposes students to the work of anthropologists, historians, sociologists, geographers, and archaeologists. But more than that, it shows how technology can be used to make students think. As you become adept at using computers, you may find yourself doing wonderfully inventive and enriching projects.

Spreadsheets play a major role in math and business. Using a computer, you can become familiar with accounting and bookkeeping, of course, but learning to use spreadsheets also exposes you to many crucial mathematical principles as well as to practical applications of math. If you were creating a budget for your future college expenses, for instance, an electronic spreadsheet would enable you to build several models of a budget, each one taking into account such variables as the cost of tuition, the distance from home, income from a part-time job, possibilities of financial aid, and so forth. If you were planning to buy a car, you would have to consider other variables such as the fluctuating cost of gasoline, expected driving mileage, cost of repairs and insurance premiums, and a host of other expenses. In other words, computer applications can be more than academic exercises; they can help you think in a mature way about some of life's major decisions.

CAD (computer-aided design) programs have awakened many students' interest in architecture, engineering, and design. Using such programs, students are drawing professional-looking plans for buildings and houses, machines, boats, automobiles and everyday objects found around the house. Corel Draw is one of many computer programs for artists. Instead of pencil and paper, artists use the monitor screen and a mouse to draw and illustrate. If you aspire to work in any area of the visual arts, including advertising and filmmaking, you should most certainly acquaint yourself with computers and their special effects techniques and capabilities. Although your school is not likely to own the sophisticated, high-tech electronic equipment being used on TV or in Hollywood, your digital education should begin with an ordinary desktop computer.

If the computer you are using has a CD-ROM player installed, you have the potential to engage in thousands of new learning experiences. CD-ROM's try to combine the best of books and videos. They often succeed. If you are studying films, for example, the CD-ROM *Cinemania,* published by Microsoft, lets you read what the critics wrote about 150 of the all-time best movies. But you can also see still photos, hear famous lines spoken aloud, and view videoclips from many of them.

The selection of educational CD-ROM's is varied and growing rapidly. While the content of most CD-ROM's relates to a specific subject, such as literature, history or art, others are general reference works. Microsoft's *Bookshelf* alone contains the *Concise Columbia Encyclopedia, The American Heritage Dictionary, Roget's Thesaurus,* an almanac and book of facts, *Bartlett's Familiar Quotations* and a world atlas all on one disk. With such CD-ROM titles as *U.S. Civics, The Washington Times Insight on the News, Think For Yourself, History of Art, Jeux d'Images Multimedia, Physical Science: Machines & Mechanics,* and many others, it should be apparent that mere browsing will expose you to ideas and information to stimulate your mind and add to your storehouse of knowledge.

PRESENTING YOUR WORK

Earlier in this book, you were encouraged to make your work look gorgeous before handing it in to your teacher. Although it may seem petty, the appearance of a paper or project often influences the grade you'll receive.

If you have access to a computer, there is no excuse for submitting anything that does not look sharp. With a desktop publishing program such as PageMaker or Ready, Set, Go (RSG), you can prepare pages that look as though a graphic designer had a hand in their creation. Word processors and laser printers, some of them able to print in any color, can give your work the appearance of a professionally printed manuscript.

With the right software, you have the potential to make displays and presentations that will impress your teacher and make your classmates envy your creative talent. PowerPoint, a popular and inexpensive Microsoft program, enables you to create any number of dramatic lettering and design effects. You have the capability of having words and letters dance, roll, rock and hop around on the screen. You can zoom in on an object and then zoom out. Shapes can blink on and off and be altered as you like. You can fade out of one display and fade into the next. Photographs and text can be incorporated in any configuration you choose, and if you would like to add background narration or musical accompaniment, that, too, can be done.

The next time you are assigned an oral report or a lengthy paper to write, ask your teacher for permission to do a multimedia presentation instead. There may be occasions when a PowerPoint show may be a welcome alternative to classroom business as usual.

SUGGESTIONS FOR GETTING STARTED

First, make yourself familiar with the computer equipment in your school. Learn how the different programs work, what their limitations and advantages are. Then use the computers at school regularly and frequently, so that you become adept and find them easy to use.

When it comes time to buy your own computer equipment, be sure to weigh the costs. Prices vary, of course, and depend largely on the speed, memory, and options. If you don't already own a computer, you probably will in the near future. In college a computer may be a piece of standard equipment. You'll be expected to have one. Your dorm room may be out-fitted with the wiring needed to connect your computer to the local campus network as well as to the Internet.

If you soon expect to be in the market for a computer, here is a list of suggestions to consider as you choose it.

1. What is the name of the computer? What are the name, address, and phone number of the manufacturer?
2. Does the manufacturer offer customer service on a hotline? Do you know anyone who has had experience using the hotline? Was the service good?
3. How big is the computer's memory? Is it possible to add more memory in the future? At what cost? To run complicated programs with sound and move-ment requires many MB (megabytes) of memory. Is the computer you have in mind capable of doing what you want it to?
4. What components will you need? The basics are a computer, a keyboard, a mouse and a monitor. What about a printer? The cost of printers varies consider-ably. A scanner? A modem? A CD-ROM player? Speakers? A surge protector? Do you have a desk or table on which to put your equipment? What will be the total cost for all the hardware?

5. Does the computer come with software installed? Is it software that you want, or will you be paying for programs that you'll never use?
6. Will all components be installed by the seller, or is installation up to you? How much does it cost to have your computer made ready to plug in and use?
7. Do you know anyone who owns the model you are considering? If so, can you try it out for a few hours? If not, can you rent one from the computer store for a trial run?

If you soon expect to be buying software, here is a list of suggestions to think about as you select it.

1. What is the name of the software? What are the publisher's name, address, and phone numbers?
2. Does the publisher offer help on a hotline? Do you know anyone who has had experience using the hotline? Was the service good?
3. Are the installation and operating manuals clearly written, easy to understand, and properly indexed?
4. What is the cost of the program? Are returns possible? Rebates? Updates?
5. Is the software for a Macintosh or for a PC? How much memory must the computer have to run the program?
6. For what subjects and in what ways can this program be used to help you in your schoolwork?
7. Do you know anyone who owns the program you are considering? If so, can you try it out for a few hours? If not, will the store sell you the program on approval (i.e., you may return the program if you are not satisfied)?

Chapter 16

Tests and Examinations: The Big Score

TRUE CONFESSIONS

1. A practice SAT I (Scholastic Assessment Test) is being given to your class next week. How will you prepare for it? Is it possible to study for a test that measures your intelligence and potential?

    We recommend that you rent a movie, relax with an enjoyable book, and get a good night's sleep before the test. What do you think of this advice?

2. Sir Walter Raleigh wrote, "In examinations, those who do not wish to know ask questions of those who cannot tell." Does that statement describe the dynamics that exist between your teachers and you? What are the real purposes of tests? Would the education system be improved if examinations were abolished?

3. Chris B. was fairly confident about her performance on both the verbal and math sections of the SAT I she took last Saturday. She had finished the test with time to spare, and on those questions about which she was unsure, she guessed. Imagine her shock, therefore, when she got a very low score. She didn't know that guessing on the SAT I works against you. Chris didn't know the strategies for doing well on the exam.

    Has something like this ever happened to you? How can such a disaster be avoided?

THE NATURE OF TESTS TO COME

As you may already be aware, tests will probably be a part of your life from now on. They have been part of education for many years and are finding their way beyond the classroom, into business, industry, government, and the armed forces. Tests are used to measure fitness for entrance into college, for entrance into professional schools and training programs, and for promotions in business, industry, and the military. These tests will measure aptitude, critical thinking, and knowledge of specific topics. Obviously, doing well on such tests is important.

Most general aptitude tests ask questions that test your knowledge of words and your ability to see logical relationships. Perhaps the best way to improve your skills for this kind of test is to increase the size of your vocabulary (etymology is helpful here) by studying words, how they are used, and what they mean. There are also several practice books available to help you study for these tests; usually, the titles of these books will name the test they help you prepare for.

Tests of specific achievement are easier to prepare for; merely study the areas being covered in the tests. Review your knowledge of mathematics if you are taking a math test, or refresh your memory of Spanish, chemistry, or English grammar, and so on. It pays to be prepared.

Students bound for college will face SAT I or the ACT. SAT I is divided into two parts: (1) verbal, which tests your ability to deal with reading subjects; and (2) mathematical, which indicates your skill in dealing with numbers. Since it has been proved that success in learning depends more and more upon the ability to read with understanding, comprehension plays a large part in the verbal test. The mathematics test attempts to measure your ability to apply given concepts to new situations, that is, your ability to reason. The best preparation for SAT I (verbal) is a background of vocabulary interest, wide reading, and practice in clear thinking.

The ACT (American College Test) is also a multiple-choice exam. It contains four parts: English, Math, Reading, and Science Reasoning. The English test assesses your mastery of usage and mechanics, including punctuation, basic grammar and usage, and sentence structure. It also tests rhetorical skills, such as writing strategy, organization, and style. The Mathematics test measures knowledge of algebra, geometry, and trigonometry, The Reading test measures your ability to understand materials similar to those read in college courses, and includes passages of prose fiction and nonfiction from the fields of the humanities, social sciences, and natural sciences. The Science Reasoning test assesses your ability to think like a scientist. On the test you must answer questions about sets of scientific information presented in various formats.

To prepare for the ACT, review your math and English skills. Because the reading and science sections of the exam are more like aptitude tests than achievement tests, they are more difficult to prepare for. Reasoning skills do not improve overnight. But it will serve you well to become familiar with the format of the exam. Get a test preparation book and practice answering the questions. The more time you have to prepare before the exam, the better off you are—if you use the time profitably.

College entrance achievement tests administered by the College Board are also given on specific subject material. Known as SAT II Subject Tests, they lend themselves to a certain amount of preparation. SAT IIs are offered in many subjects. The colleges you apply to will often ask you to take them, but even if you are not required to take SAT IIs, high scores will enhance your college application. If possible, take SAT IIs in your best subjects. Many colleges ask applicants to take SAT II in Writing, which tests, among other things, your ability to write a short essay. Using a test preparation guide such as that published by Barron's will help you prepare for the exam and give you practice in writing an essay in only twenty minutes.

ATTITUDE: THE FIRST STEP

Dr. Francis P. Robinson in his book, *Effective Study,* poses this question: "Did you ever thank a teacher for giving an examination?" At first glance you are not likely to find much in your thinking that would help generate an affirmative answer. The teacher does spend much time preparing the test questions; after you have taken the examination, the teacher spends many hours carefully evaluating your paper. Mistakes are marked so that when your paper is returned you can go over them and perhaps write in corrections so you will not make the same mistakes again.

Do you consider the test or examination as a personal battle which the teacher wages in an attempt to defeat you, or as a contest in which one tries to outwit the other? If this is your attitude toward tests and examinations, you probably do one of two things when the teacher returns your paper to you. One, you throw it away without bothering to do more than glance through it to see where points were taken off; or two, without checking an incomplete answer against the facts as studied, you approach the teacher and ask why points were taken off. This is the most negative of approaches. The difference in attitude can be seen in the difference between two questions: "Why did you take off points on this question?" and "What should I have included which I did not?"

Another attitude that you should avoid is that of fear. Fear of taking tests and examinations results in tension and disturbed thinking, which produce blind spots (not being able to remember answers that you knew ten minutes before the test) and careless mistakes. This fear also keeps people from venturing into new areas in life. They may visualize the new method, the better tool, or the strong bridge, but they hesitate until someone else realizes their dreams.

Fear prevents success on tests and examinations because fear conditions the mind for failure. Students who are afraid start in a state of confusion and disorder; thus they throw away the advantages they have accumulated by preparation. Students who approach tests and examinations with fear are almost always characterized by the following: (1) Their mark is considerably lower than they expected. (2) They complain about the teacher—insufficient explanation, lack of detailed review, etc. (3) They find fault with the test material—too long, not the type of questions expected and studied for, didn't understand the wording of questions, read the word *muckrakers* instead of *mugwumps* and missed the whole point. (4) Their preparation consists of a frantic last-ditch effort, loss of sleep almost to the point of total exhaustion, and often loss of important notes or review material just when they were needed most.

If you recognize two or more of these characteristics as behavior patterns which you practice at test and examination time, try to change your attitude as quickly as possible. To continue them is to subject yourself to a climate of tension and fear and to condition yourself for defeat.

A third attitude is wholly positive. It is the attitude of challenge, self-confidence, and content-reliability. Students who accept a test as a challenge to show the teacher the extent of their knowledge of the subject and to improve their grades are stimulated. This stimulation produces the energy needed to think clearly and to act with precision. The attitude of challenge is reflected by enterprising rather than burdensome preparation, and self-confidence develops from this adequate preparation. There is no room for tension and fear. Even a questionable answer is approached by a calculated reliability that a worthwhile answer, although perhaps only partially correct, can be worked out. This attitude requires the relationship between student and teacher, and question and answer, always to be one of cooperative production rather than competitive destruction.

LEARNING FROM TESTS

Tests provide opportunities both for your teachers to evaluate your knowledge and skills, and for you to learn. Many students think only of the first aspect of testing and never realize the value tests have in helping them learn.

From tests you can learn what your weaknesses are in a subject and take steps to correct them. Do you make errors in reading questions? Take the time to be more careful in reading. Do you find the questions ask about things you didn't think were important? You may overcome this problem with practice in asking yourself questions about topics, and in making your questions similar to the ones your teacher asks. Do you find your notes do not contain information on which you were tested? Be more alert for key ideas in class—learn from the questions on tests what kind of information your teacher considers important. Make sure that you have that kind of information in your notes. Do you find that your teacher reviewed material for the test but that you did not pay attention? Help yourself by active listening, especially in the time just before a test.

All of these suggestions for learning from tests require that you review your tests when your teacher hands them back. It is foolish to discard a test in anger and not try to learn from your mistakes.

Tests will also give you practice in writing. You will gain practice in organizing essays, in deciding the importance of ideas, and in expressing ideas. To improve your performance in these writing skills, learn from your mistakes. Pay attention to what your teacher writes about your essays and strive to avoid repeating those kinds of mistakes.

REVIEWING FOR TESTS AND EXAMINATIONS

The most successful review is the one that starts with the second assignment at the beginning of the term and continues as a part of daily preparation throughout the course. Such a review should include a well-organized notebook, a basic vocabulary for the course, important class notes, all weekly and monthly test questions, and a well-marked textbook, indicating the material designated important during the course. In addition, a mental blueprint should be woven into the material, uniting the parts of the subject into a unified whole.

This procedure cannot be stressed too strongly; the student who fails to follow it usually faces an impossible task a week or two before the examination. We all know how complex and difficult it is to learn even a small amount of material thoroughly; thus, the person who attempts a whole term's work in a week is playing a silly, losing game. If your continuous review is carried out from week to week, preparing for a weekly quiz or a monthly test should require no more time than a regular daily assignment; an hour test should not demand more than two hours of review. Your test review should deal largely with class work or lab work rather than rereading. Check main topics for recall; where main headings draw a blank, do a limited amount of rereading. This, plus careful attention to important questions and hints given by the teacher, should complete your quiz and test preparation. Therefore, suggestions for review which follow are directed mainly toward the final examination. Several of the practices can be adapted for use in preparing for smaller tests.

Examinations demand primarily the recall of large amounts of information. The objective examination requires only recall; the essay examination demands recall plus organization and amplification. Since effective recall depends upon study distributed over a long period of time, even your immediate review for an examination should be divided into hourly periods of study which start ten days or two weeks before the examination. Review should never be started later than a week before the exam. Five one-hour review periods spread over five days are far more beneficial than ten hours of attempted study the day before the examination.

A ten-hour session or a five-hour ordeal the day before the examination, or an all-night period of mental exhaustion and confusion, cannot be considered review. It can only be described as a short-sighted, superficial, and futile struggle to cram a great deal of information into one's mind. At most, cramming provides a smattering of information for short-term use only. The information slips away quickly, usually even before the examination can be finished. Its chief function is to overlay what you have learned during the term with confusion. It is far better to read a good book, go to a movie, get a good night's sleep, and appear at the exam feeling well-rested and energetic.

Pages could be written on the disastrous effects of cramming; the case histories of its ill results and failure would fill volumes. Let us leave its senselessness and learn ways to make a review less a period of self-torture and more a period of profitable study.

SUGGESTIONS FOR SUCCESSFUL REVIEW

➤ Learn to select what is most important to learn. General principles, formulas and experimental conclusions, vocabularies and rules, historical sequences and literary types, and theories and facts are some of the important items in your courses. Be sure to differentiate between opinion and fact. Pay particular attention to material that is emphasized by boldface type, questions, or repeated in summary paragraphs.

➤ Listen with such precision during the two weeks before the examination that you miss nothing that is said in class. Even though the teacher may be continuing with new material, there are signs to indicate that important items for review are being made available to you. Listen for such statements as: "In October we studied a case not unlike this one. Remember why it was considered so important." "This is the eighth essential principle we have studied this term. They are all important to an understanding of the course." Teachers often refer in one way or another to almost everything you will see on the examination. Listen for it.

It is also important to keep your eyes open. Remember the story of the teacher who filled the board with French and English sentences, vocabulary words, rates, etc., a week before examination time. Nothing was said to explain why all this had been written there, and no one asked. When the students saw the examination, the truth was self-evident. The examination had been on the blackboard for a whole week. Two students smiled and began writing perfect papers; they had seen. The others had looked too, but had seen nothing; they each got about their expected grade.

➤ Review by using questions to predict questions. When you have found what you consider important, turn it into a question, or ask yourself how it could be made into a question. This requires discipline, for many students choose the easy method of forming only questions which they know they can answer. However, the easy questions are never the only ones asked on examinations. Be honest; accept the hard ones and prepare answers. Good students can predict close to 90 percent of an examination.

Do not confuse prediction that results from thorough study with a guessing game. It does not mean simply trying to outguess the teacher, and doing only spot studying. This is usually fatal. You have often heard the victim lament, "I thought he was going to ask

_____ , but he didn't, so I had to blank four whole questions."

➤ Review by reorganizing your course material. Where possible, reduce the subject matter to easily remembered divisions .In mathematics these divisions may be definitions, word problems, theorems, formulas, and general concepts. In history they may be biography, chronology, reform movements (radical), reform movements (conservative), domestic wars, foreign wars, economic problems, civic problems, and religious problems. This is one of the most profitable of all review procedures. At first glance it may appear to hinder unity and continuity of the subject. However, it does just the opposite; it binds the parts of the course into a more workable and understandable unit.

➤ Review by changing your point of view. If you have dealt with a subject during the term from the point of view of memorization to receive a credit only, change your point of view to that of application for understanding. The first point of view is a deterrent to successful study; the second is one of study's greatest psychological aids. And unless your mind is prepared, there can be no profitable review.

Change your point of view from that of observer to participant. If you are reviewing history, put yourself into character. Accept a role—not the king, the general, or the hero—through which you can get a comprehensive feeling for the people you are studying. Be a slave, a common soldier, a person in the street. If you are reviewing a foreign language, imagine that in six weeks you will be allowed to use only this language.

Reviewing by changing your point of view can be an exciting game. Use your imagination and find new approaches to all your subjects.

➤ Make question "terminology" and question "reading" a part of your review. Although certain words appear in question after question, these key words often mean different things to different teachers. You must know what the teacher expects when the question says *explain, evaluate, state, relate, illustrate, enumerate, describe, interpret, define, diagram, compare, contrast, compare and contrast.* Practice reading chapter-end questions to understand exactly what a question asks for. Note the characteristics of questions that pertain to different subjects. Some subjects lend themselves to specifics; questions in other subjects are very general. Question knowledge should be an important part of any review.

TAKING TESTS AND EXAMINATIONS

Tests and examinations are generally of two kinds: objective and subjective. Objective, or short-answer, tests require you to recognize correct answers among incorrect ones, or true statements set beside false ones. Objective tests also measure your ability to recall details. Objective questions are usually one of the following types: (1) Recall (filling in blanks): Joseph Conrad was born in _____ and spent his early years _____ . (2) Recognition (multiple choice): Gandhi learned of civil disobedience from (a) Emerson (b) Gladstone (c) Lincoln (d) Marx (e) Thoreau. Ans. (   ) True or False questions are also considered recognition questions: Mockingbirds belong to the mimic family. (T) Mockingbirds belong to the sparrow family. (F) A third type of recognition question is the matching question. For example, write the number of the phrase which fits the character in the space provided:

1.	Founder of Hebrew Nation	_2_	Lincoln
2.	The Great Emancipator	_1_	Moses
3.	Apostle of Peace	_4_	Gladstone
4.	Three times Prime Minister	_5_	Einstein
5.	Scientist and Philosopher	_3_	Woodrow Wilson

Here are some things that you should consider in approaching objective examinations.

➤ Pay particular attention to mechanical instructions; that is, instructions that tell you *where* and *how* to answer questions. Wrong position may result in wrong answers; in any case, answering in ways other than that required may cause the teacher difficulty in grading your paper. Some teachers take off points when instructions are not followed.

➤ Make a quick survey of the whole test before writing any answer. Get an overview to help you determine how quickly you will need to work.

➤ The questions are usually numerous; sometimes you do not have to answer all of them. Always answer the questions that you know first and come back to any that you wish to spend time on.

➤ Read certain types of objective questions (particularly True-False) so that you observe all qualifying words. These words—*usually, always, most, never, some*— give insight into when and under what conditions a statement is or is not correct. Modifiers play their most important role in True-False questions.

➤ All objective questions require correct reading. Don't let premeditated opinion cause you to read into the question a word that is not there. This results in wrong answers, and after the examination you are heard to say, "But I thought the question was . . ."

➤ Do not change answers too quickly as you check your examination before turning it in. Your first answer might be more reliable unless you are absolutely sure you have made a mistake. If there is any doubt, leave the first answer.

➤ Do not think that neatness and order can be ignored on objective examinations. Words and numbers can be written sloppily or neatly. Neatness begins with the first blank you fill and ends with the way you sign your name.

The second kind of test, the subjective, demands more of the student in both recalling and organizing subject matter. These are usually called *essay* tests; they may be short-answer questions (a paragraph) or discussion questions (a lengthy essay which measures the student's entire scope of knowledge on a particular part of the course). The word *subjective* implies that this kind of examination is more personal than the objective test. It provides students with a greater opportunity to show the extent of their preparation. It also provides the teacher with a chance to make more personal judgments in evaluating the paper. For this reason you should think in terms of what judgment you would make of your answers if you were the teacher.

Essay examinations measure your ability to recall what you have learned, organize it intelligently, and express it clearly and with meaningful interpretation, selection, or application, depending upon what is asked for. The first and most important thing to remember about essay examination questions is that there is no such thing as a *general answer.*

You can write successful essay examinations by practicing a few *must* requirements:

➤ Read through all the essay questions before you start to write and allot time to each question. Divide the time available for the test according to the importance of the questions. A question that is worth 25 percent of the test should get 25 percent of the available time.

➤ Read the question to determine exactly what it asks you to do and what instructions are included for doing it. If the question asks for Alexander's spiritual legacy, it is a waste of time to describe the physical legacy (army, devoted generals, etc.) he received from his father. As in objective questions, qualifying words give the question its explicit meaning. Yet some students misread questions. The students who read *conservationists* instead of *conservatives* may write a beautiful answer, but they will get no credit; they answered a question that wasn't asked. The qualifying words of a question are really the directions for answering it. A record of careless mistakes on tests and examinations made by students at Kent School over a five-year period showed that carelessness in reading the question was responsible for 64 percent of all careless mistakes.

➤ Read the first question you are going to answer and write a brief outline of your major points in the margin. Think for a minute or two about your answer to check the arrangement of ideas. Make sure your answer includes all important ideas. THINKING BEFORE WRITING will improve your essays as nothing else will.

➤ As you write, restate the question if you can, but at least make the subject of the question the subject of your answer. Never start an answer with a pronoun without an antecedent. Two such beginnings, fatal to a good mark but often used, are "It is when" and "It is because." Always make the subject of the question the subject of your answer. As you read the question for the second time you must constantly watch for anything that will give your answer an element of vagueness.

➤ As you write your answer keep in mind the teacher's preference for style of presentation, use of illustration to show understanding, and elements of a model answer. If the teacher has complimented you on earlier test papers for the way you handled an answer, try to apply this method to as many questions as possible. Ask yourself the question, "What is the teacher's aim in this particular question?" Make your paper easy to mark. Use signal words and numerals to introduce important facts and series. Number questions to the left of the red margin and skip one or two lines between answers. Remember that the neatly written paper has fewer mistakes and is easier for the teacher to mark.

➤ Concentrate on one question at a time, and use a mental system of numbering important points in your answer. Students often overwrite or write away from questions because they jump ahead and are thinking of a question to come. The teacher has not asked questions that require repeating subject matter, so be careful to keep all answers within the limits set by the questions. An excellent method for avoiding generalizations and worthless padding is to mentally number important points as you write them down. Illustrations, specific elaboration, important facts, and explanations to clarify your understanding of a definition or event are all necessary parts of a good essay answer. If you number important items mentally as you write, you will see the difference between what has value (and will add to your mark) and what is worthless.

➤ Check over the completed examination paper before you turn it in. You should reserve ten minutes of each examination hour for checking after you have completed the writing. Check for mechanical errors and obvious factual mistakes such as wrong words, incorrect conclusions, transposed characters, etc. As with objective tests, do not change anything in an answer unless you are absolutely sure it is wrong. Rely on your first impression.

➤ You can learn much about writing better examinations and using better methods of study by going over the graded paper after it has been returned. By checking against your book you can see what you omitted that the teacher considered important or how you misinterpreted the qualifying word in a question. If you note such errors carefully, you will not repeat them on the next test.

SUMMARY OF RULES FOR REVIEWING FOR AND TAKING TESTS AND EXAMINATIONS

1. Review by selecting the important subject matter; concentrate on it rather than on the trivial and incidental.
2. Review by listening for hints and helps given by the teacher just prior to the test.
3. Review by predicting questions for the test. Think how questions can be asked on specific subject matter.
4. Review by reorganizing the subject matter into logical divisions. Keep a sense of unity by being aware of relationships among parts.

5. Review by changing your point of view. Let your imagination add interest to the subject.

6. Review by knowing what *question words* mean. Learn what your teacher expects when certain key words are used.

7. When you take the test or examination, read all questions and instructions carefully and repeatedly until you understand exactly what the answer and the presentation of the answer require.

8. Know the general implications of key and qualifying words in both objective and essay questions. Do not, under any circumstances, make an exception for what the qualifying word asks for.

9. On objective tests give the precise answer; on essay tests give the complete answer. Always remember that quantity without quality will not get a good grade.

10. Observe all rules of neatness, mechanics, and clarity. The attractive paper that is easy to read gets the better grade.

11. Check your paper carefully before you turn it in. Unless you are absolutely sure you have made a mistake, do not change your answers. The first impression, as psychological tests have shown, is more reliable.

12. Improve all future test and examination grades by carefully checking all returned papers. Note your errors and shortcomings so you will not repeat them on the next test.

LOOKING BACK

1. What do teachers and test makers mean when they ask you to do the following?

    a. Evaluate
    b. Describe
    c. Compare and contrast

2. Some baseball batters are guess hitters. They guess at the kind of pitch that will be thrown to them (fast ball, curve, slider, change of pace) and then swing. Should you guess about test questions your teacher is likely to ask and prepare for them exclusively?

    Do you study with a friend who knows more or less than you do? What are the advantages and disadvantages of studying for a test with a friend?

3. One proven tip for test takers is to check their paper over thoroughly before submitting it to the teacher. List three additional tips you found in this chapter. What suggestion, if any, could you make that was not mentioned in this chapter?

Chapter 17

Motivation: Each Must Find It For Oneself

THE REACH AND THE GRASP

"Ah, but a man's reach should exceed his grasp, Or what's a heaven for?" Thus wrote Robert Browning in his poem, "Andrea del Sarto," in 1855. Although what is within one's reach today has multiplied beyond the vaguest dream of anyone living in Browning's day, it is still a part of natural law that unless one's dreams exceed what one is momentarily capable of grasping, one stops learning. One's life becomes mere survival; finally one is pushed off the stage by a better actor who has developed a greater capacity to reach for dreams. William Golding makes this point in an exciting book entitled *The Inheritors,* in which he describes how slow-witted Neanderthal man was replaced by a person capable of greater vision—Cro-Magnon man.

"But what has this to do with me?" you ask. Beginning with your endowments and the gifts that grow from these endowments, we have encompassed all of the best study methods and practices. They are within both your grasp and your reach to improve your grades. However, if you are really going to succeed, you must extend the demands you make upon these learning processes to drive you from what you are toward what you can become.

This factor, which determines success or failure both in school and in life, is elusive, difficult to isolate from the whole of one's character, and also impossible to define. It is a combination of interest, ambition, inspiration, moral acceptance of life's importance, a sense of values, and faith in oneself. It is sometimes called by one of the several parts ascribed to it, but generally it is given a name which suggests forward movement and the rhythm of a firm, quick step—*motivation.*

The power of motivation lies in striving to be the best, not in merely appearing so. Without motivation, people atrophy and civilizations decline. You can ponder forever what makes one person succeed and another fail. But if you were asked why a great civilization declines, you might answer, "A great civilization declines not because geography changes but because people's minds change." People become satisfied and cease to be excited about learning. Civilization declines when people do not want to do and to know; when work becomes drudgery and love of learning is replaced by resentment and impatience; when the aim of learning becomes social status rather than truth and ennoblement.

What do we really know of this moving purpose, motivation, that so profoundly affects people and nations? First, we should remind ourselves that motivation is that which strives for what is excellent. Perhaps we can find how much of the whole concept of motivation is within us by looking at some of its components.

What can all the study methods in the world do for you if you lack interest? No one can be interested for you; your parents cannot wish it upon you; your teachers cannot force it upon you. Interest is the basic obligation that you must carry into each classroom. Interest often transforms subject matter from something very dead into something active and alive.

Interest gives work a new dimension. Tom Sawyer discovered it when he had his friends whitewash the fence for him. "Work," he said, "consists of whatever a body is obliged to do, and play consists of whatever a body is not obliged to do." Interest gives obligation the quality and character of privilege. You can use interest to take the feeling of compulsion out of study. Interest will help you do more and better work than is required. The clockwatcher finds the day long and seemingly endless. The interested worker never has all the time he or she wants. Perhaps interest, as a component of motivation, is best summed up by an old axiom that has long hung on the walls of a classroom at Kent School: "If a man does only what is required of him he is a slave; the moment he does more he is a free man."

What of the ingredient of motivation we call ambition? It is far more than simple willingness to receive. Alexander the Great, at the age of twenty, inherited a well-equipped army led by brilliant and devoted generals. If Alexander had been content only to receive, the army would have belonged to the generals.

Ambition, like the other ingredients of motivation, can be measured by the drop or by the barrel. It is within your power to inventory whatever ambition is within you. Only you can add up your resources, color them by bold strokes with the brush of imagination, and hold them before you as a bright picture of your abilities.

It is easy to make a check list of your ambitions concerning your school work. In addition, much that will pertain to your life's ambitions should be put on your check list while you are still in school.

1. What are my abilities?
2. What will my ambition require of me?

3. What will success mean in the career or job for which I aim?
4. What will defeat mean?
5. Have I put the proper value upon my life and my time?
6. Will my work provide sufficient inspiration and challenge to save me from complacency and stagnation?

We could continue through some explanation of all the components of motivation, but by now you should see what is happening. We have come full circle and are talking about your gifts as described in Chapter 1. Thus, the only way to understand the meaning of motivation is to understand your own gifts and the uses to which they can be put.

Don't stand still if you can walk; don't walk if you can run; don't run if you can fly. There is an old Indian legend of an eaglet that thought it was a prairie chicken and never used its wings. As the story goes, an Indian boy found an eagle's egg and put it in a prairie chicken's nest. The eaglet hatched with the brood of prairie chicks and grew up with them. The changeling eagle, thinking it was a prairie chicken, did what prairie chickens did. It scratched in the dirt for seeds and insects to eat, never flew more than a short distance, and that with an awkward flutter of wings, only a few feet off the ground. After all, that's how prairie chickens were supposed to fly.

Then one day when the eagle was grown, it saw a magnificent bird far above it in the sky. Riding with graceful majesty on the powerful wind currents, it soared with scarcely a beat of its golden wings.

"What a beautiful bird!" said the eagle to one of the prairie chickens. "What is it?"

"That's an eagle, the chief of birds," the prairie chicken replied. "But don't give it a second thought. You could never fly like it."

So the eagle never gave it a second thought, never rose beyond the brief thrashing of wings and the flurry of feathers, and grew old, and died thinking it was a prairie chicken. It's all too easy to go through life thinking we're prairie chickens when we're really eagles.

MOTIVATION—IMPERISHABLE

Let us conclude with two true stories to illustrate a fact: if you show concern for both the better self of which you are capable and your gifts through which you can achieve this better self, motivation will take care of itself.

Not all your papers will be returned with honor grades. When you have done your best and still get a low grade, there will be moments of discouragement, doubt, and depression. When this happens, remind yourself of the following story.

The first scene of the story is set in the wilderness of Indiana. A small boy trudges through the winter forest to a one-room school. After six weeks the school closed and the boy suffered the first of many deeply felt disappointments. By the time he was twenty-two, he had wandered as an itinerant worker and was now a partner in a crossroads store at the edge of a frontier village in Illinois. The store failed and he lost every penny he had saved from seven years' hard labor.

The lesson had been expensive, but he felt that he had learned by hard experience. He would not fail again. Two years of struggle provided him with enough funds to enter a second partnership. This time he would succeed. But within two years the second store had failed. The young man's partner drank up the profits. The person to whom the partners sold the store failed to make his payments, and when the entire stock of goods had been sold, disappeared with the receipts. When the former partner died the young man was left with debts which seemed impossible to ever pay off.

Now he asked a friend to help him get a job as a surveyor, and he studied mathematics with the village schoolmaster to prepare himself for the job. After he was appointed to the surveyor's job, he borrowed money to buy instruments and a horse; however, he never had a chance to begin work. Creditors from his mercantile failures seized his possessions and he lost both horse and instruments.

Immediately after this the gods dealt him the cruelest blow of all, convincing him that he had been singled out for pain and failure from birth. His sweetheart, perhaps a deep and enduring love, the like of which he did not experience again, suddenly died. He descended to the depths of despair and gloom, often pondering whether the struggle to live was worth it. Long afterward he wrote, "At this period of my life I never dared to carry a pocketknife, fearing I would destroy myself."

Time passes. The man no longer looks young, although he is not yet forty. After ten years of struggle he has paid off the last of his debts. While he worked to pay them off, he also spent long hours trying to satisfy his insatiable hunger to be able to put into words what he felt, to understand the feelings of men around him.

Friends began to suggest that this failure might be a success in the most unexpected of places—politics. So they elected him to Congress. He did not succeed; after two short terms he was defeated for reelection. Nine years later his staunch friends determined to nominate him for the U.S. Senate. However, a split developed in the party and he was forced to step aside in favor of a candidate who could win the number of votes for nomination. This too was failure. Two years later, when he did manage to be nominated and run for the Senate, he was soundly defeated. Of this failure he said, "I was down and out of politics at the age of 50." Looking back over thirty years of his life he could not claim a single personal victory.

The motivating forces of gods and men, of fate, of dreams and destiny, are beyond prediction and comprehension. No man knows when he is walking with destiny, and no man was ever less suspecting than this long-time loser. For in the fifty-second year of life, in the thirty-second year of failure, this man was elected President of the United States. He is usually listed among the half-dozen greatest men who ever lived. His name, of course, is Abraham Lincoln.

MOTIVATION—A SEED FALLING UPON GOOD GROUND

The second story is really a continuation of the first. Abraham Lincoln had one thing in common with Anthony La Manna. Anthony was born on April 14; the day on which Lincoln was shot. The years were different, however; Lincoln was shot in 1865 and Anthony La Manna was born in 1888 in the village of Valguarnera Caropepe, amid the stone quarries of Monte Erei.

Anthony La Manna, one of eleven children, entered the quarries as a laborer at the age of twelve. Under the scorching Sicilian sun, amid the deafening ringing of hammers and thunderous thuds and rattles of giant slabs of stone crashing into pits, Anthony La Manna dreamed of nothing beyond the sulphur and rock-salt mines near the sea, where the pay was better. But even these mines seemed far away. They were south over the hills and past the valley through which ran the Assinarus River. Tony could wipe the sweat from his brow and scan the jagged horizon, but the hope of better wages from sulphur or rock-salt mines was far away—perhaps too far.

Few ever went from the quarries. The pattern of trudging up the mountain at sunrise and back down at sunset, with an occasional goatherd to offer news from beyond the hills, became for most the center and circumference of a world.

Anthony La Manna, reading the history of his island with his fifth-grade education, and listening to his elders talk, believed that change was against the natural order of things. Sicily, he thought, had really not changed much in the 2315 years since Nicias and the Athenian army had been destroyed on the banks of the Assinarus River in 415 B.C. The Athenians who were defeated in battle were enslaved in the quarries, where they were scorched by the sun and where they died. Anthony La Manna had also seen men die in the quarries.

When Tony La Manna was sixteen, he followed the valley and the river down to the sea. In the Gulf of Gela a ship was loading goods to carry to America, and Anthony La Manna hired on.

There were times in America when Anthony would have given much to be back on the road which led homeward from the quarry, where the friendly voice of the goatherd broke the loneliness. But his four years in the quarries had given him much skill with a chisel and a hammer on stone; after a short time of digging ditches in the swamps of New Jersey, he became a stonecutter's apprentice in Washington, D.C., and began work on the Lincoln Memorial in 1914.

Day after day, as he worked high on the scaffold, he studied the countenance on the gigantic statue. The sad, tired man, who had begun life in surroundings as humble as those of Tony La Manna, had become a lawyer, and a president. One day at lunch time, as Tony La Manna sat on the end of the high scaffold looking into the middle section of the great monument, where sat the rail splitter from the wilderness of Illinois, the stone splitter from Monte Erei made a sudden decision—Anthony La Manna could make something more of himself. He would become a lawyer. On a piece of planking he wrote "Anthony La Manna" and under his name "Attorney at Law." At the end of the day he brought the piece of board down from the scaffold. His friends laughed—"Another Aba Lincoln mayba. Tony, you looka too much at the statue."

It's a long way from a noisy fifth grade class in the little stuccoed school in Caropepe, Sicily, to the National Law Center at George Washington University in Washington, D.C. After ten hours on a scaffold with chisel and hammer, there was night school—"Engulesh, how you say in Engulesh! Noun, verb, what for pronoun, adjudgtive?" And in his canvas bag with chisels, hammer, and salami sandwiches, Tony La Manna carried books. He would hurry through his lunch and begin to read. His friends would laugh, as long before Lincoln's rail-splitting companions had laughed at him, as he sat on a stump with a book in one hand and a slab of salt pork between two chunks of cornbread in the other.

In the midst of his work on the memorial and his studying in night school, Anthony La Manna went off to fight in World War I for democracy and the right to be free and learn and become something in America. When he came back he resumed both his work on the memorial and his studies. At age thirty-two, sixteen years in America, he was chosen to carve the Gettysburg Address on the memorial. He was to inscribe these immortal words of Lincoln in stone for them to be forever enshrined in the hearts of men. While completing that task, Anthony also earned his LL.B. and LL.M.

For nearly forty years he was a successful lawyer in both New York and Washington, and was special counselor to the Veteran's Administration for thirty-two years. When asked to describe what he considered motivation, he said, "Impossible, for each man must discover and define it for himself."

So ends the story, the chapter, and this book. What is motivation and whence does it come? The answer is as difficult to describe as trying to tell the direction of the wind by hearing it move through far-off hills at night. Unless you find your own answer to what motivation is, you will never know. If you have it, you will know; if you do not have it, those around you will know

You can escape neither time nor history. Unless you use the gifts you have been given, time will close many doors which open on long corridors of opportunity through which you will never be permitted to walk. As you turn your back on the closed doors to walk in the tracks you have already made, you will find history gazing upon you, holding you accountable for misappropriation.

"Of what?" you demand.

"Of your talents," answers history.

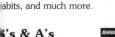

NOTES

NOTES

NOTES

NOTES

NOTES